big
data
@
work

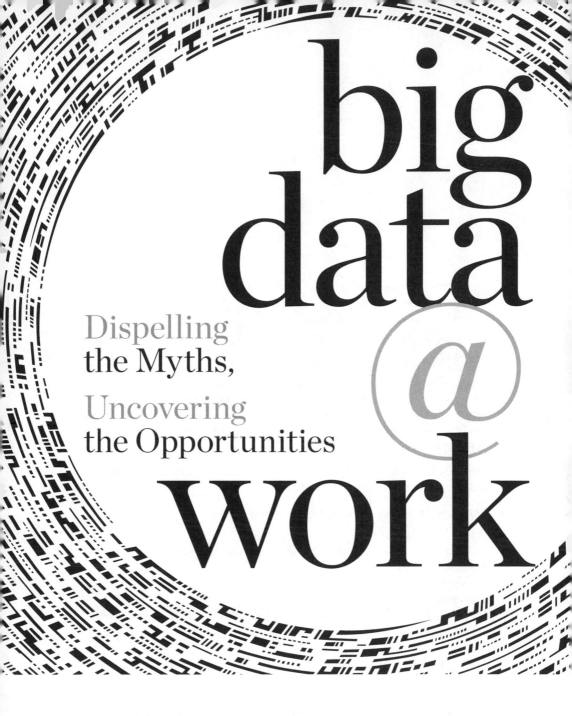

big
data
@
work

Dispelling
the Myths,

Uncovering
the Opportunities

THOMAS H. DAVENPORT

Harvard Business Review Press

Boston, Massachusetts

The web addresses referenced in this book were live and correct at the time of the
book's publication but may be subject to change.

Library of Congress Cataloging-in-Publication Data

Davenport, Thomas H., 1954-
  Big data at work : dispelling the myths, uncovering the opportunities / Thomas H.
  Davenport.
      pages cm
  ISBN 978-1-4221-6816-5 (alk. paper)
1. Business intelligence—Data processing. 2. Big data. 3. Business planning—Statistical
methods. 4. Data mining. I. Title.
  HD38.7.D379 2014
  658.4'038—dc23

                        2013039005

The paper used in this publication meets the requirements of the American National
Standard for Permanence of Paper for Publications and Documents in Libraries and
Archives Z39.48-1992.

ISBN: 9781422168165
eISBN: 9781422168172

Contents

Acknowledgments

It would be wonderful if I were smart enough to come up with the ideas in this book on my own, but I'm not. So I have to rely on the kindness and wisdom of others who share with me what they are doing with big data. I am therefore grateful to all those individuals who shared their experiences and insights with me. Every story in this book—and there are many of them—has a generous individual behind it.

I am also grateful to my friends at SAS Institute, which has sponsored much of my research on analytics. Two of the studies they sponsored are described in this book. Mike Bright is my primary contact at SAS, and Scott VanValkenburg was my first connection there. Both continue to be good friends and advisers after almost a decade of collaboration. Others at SAS deserving thanks include Ken Blank, Jim Davis, Carl Farrell, Jim Goodnight, Deb Orton, Adele Sweetwood, and too many others to mention.

I did some of the research in this book with the help of the International Institute for Analytics, which I cofounded with Jack Phillips. Thanks to Jack, Katherine Busey, Sarah Gates, Callie Youssi, and everyone else at IIA for their help.

I've been a senior adviser to Deloitte Analytics for several years now; Jane Griffin was a great supporter and friend. Thanks also to Forrest Danson, Wendy DeHoef, Kelly Nelson, Tim Phillipps, and Fred Roffman—all Deloitte Analytics folks—for their continued support. Marcus Shingles at Deloitte led a research project on big data in the

Grocery Manufacturers Association in which I participated, and some of those ideas are undoubtedly in the book as well.

Finally, I began a research project on data discovery while writing this book, and some of the research made it into the book before it was completed. Teradata Aster supported that research, and I would like to thank Tasso Argyros and Mary Gros for giving me access to their customers and product capabilities.

I also work with a number of companies and organizations as an adviser or affiliated researcher, and I learn a lot from all of them. They include, in alphabetical order, First Analytics, MarketShare, Medidata Solutions, the MIT Center for Digital Business, Mu Sigma, Real Impact, Signals Intelligence Group, and Via Science. I tell all of these organizations that my primary goal in the relationship is to learn from them, and they all have delivered on that request.

The other people who played important roles in making this book a reality are at Harvard Business Review Press. Melinda Merino has edited several of my books in the past, and she was in this case—as always—a great pleasure to work with. I can't remember for sure, but I think writing this book was her idea. Certainly she had great suggestions along the way for making it more compelling and engaging.

I have been remiss in past books in not thanking Julie Devoll, my longtime publicist at the Press. Normally I don't know who is going to publicize the book when I write the acknowledgments, but Julie assures me that I will get her expert and unflagging services on this one. If anyone hears or reads about this book, it will probably be thanks to Julie.

I love the jacket design for this book and my previous one with the Press, and that's due to the excellent work of Stephani Finks. Tracy Williams led the marketing team for the book. Allison Peter ably and smoothly handled the copyediting and artwork. Thanks also to Julia Kirby, my old friend and frequent editor at *Harvard Business Review,* for helping me clarify my thoughts on this topic in a couple of articles I wrote for the magazine.

My wife, Jodi Davenport, urged me to write a book on big data long before I actually got started. My sons, Hayes and Chase, have at least some interest in the topic as well—Hayes in terms of the entertainment industry, and Chase in terms of education. Thanks to all of them for the advice.

I have written more books than I have family, and I am now faced with rededicating books to family members. My mother-in-law, Helen Kubik, was the dedicatee for my book *Competing on Analytics*. Not only did she get more enjoyment out of the dedication than anyone else in the role does, but the book also sold quite well. So Helen, this book is dedicated to you. Work your magic again, please!

1

Why Big Data Is Important to You and Your Organization

Big data is undeniably big, but it's also a bit misnamed. It's a catchall term for data that doesn't fit the usual containers. Big data refers to data that is too big to fit on a single server, too unstructured to fit into a row-and-column database, or too continuously flowing to fit into a static data warehouse. While its size receives all the attention, the most difficult aspect of big data really involves its lack of structure.

Books like this one generally start by talking about how much data there is in the world. You know the numbers and the comparisons—the average company has 427 times the amount of data ever recorded in the Library of Congress. Facebook has more photographic data than all the pixels ever processed by Kodak. We capture more video daily than the first fifty years of television. These aren't real facts about the dazzling nature of data volumes and types today—I made them up— but they're probably not that far off.

I haven't started with this kind of recitation because I don't think it matters much. Yes, there is a massive amount of data out there; according to one study, the world used over 2.8 zettabytes of data (that's 2.8 trillion gigabytes—of course, an unfathomably large number) in 2012.[1] Yes, it's more than anything we have ever known, and it will only become more voluminous over time. But although mentioning how much data we have may be useful for cocktail parties, to organizations that need to manage and take advantage of big data, the total volume isn't the point. We might even use the old cliché (from another context), "Size doesn't matter."

The point is not to be dazzled by the volume of data, but rather to analyze it—to convert it into insights, innovations, and business value. The study cited previously suggests that only .5 percent of the 2.8 zettabytes of data is analyzed in any way. The greatest barrier to analysis is that we first have to impose structure on big data; most of those 2.8 zettabytes are not currently in row-and-column formats. We have a huge task ahead of us—to start structuring the data, analyzing it, and getting value from it. Not all of it will be useful—the study estimates about 25 percent has potential value—but whatever the number, we are only scratching the surface of what's possible.

Beyond the Big Data Hype

You should be skeptical about big data and all the hype that accompanies it. I know I was, at least until I started researching the topic. I'd done a lot of work with companies on the use of analytics in business, and had written several books on the topic, including *Competing on Analytics* (with Jeanne Harris) and *Analytics at Work* (with Jeanne Harris and Bob Morison). I'd worked with well over a hundred companies on how to use analytics for competitive advantage. I confess that I initially thought that big data was simply old analytics wine poured into a new bottle. The term started to take off in the fourth quarter of 2010, and there weren't many examples yet outside of Silicon Valley. So I assumed it was just another example of vendor, consultant, and technology analyst hype. I briefly considered taking my books on *analytics,* doing a global replacement with the term *big data,* and—voilà!—several new books (kidding!).

I discovered that I was wrong to be skeptical after I began doing research on the topic in 2011. I undertook several systematic studies, including one on data scientists and the human factor in big data, one on big data in big companies, one on big data in the travel industry, and one on the data discovery process in big data.[2] I did over a hundred interviews for these projects in big data start-ups, established online firms, and large companies in traditional industries. In large, established businesses, it wasn't uncommon for managers to share my skepticism and distrust of the hype. They often felt that they had been dealing with big data for years (at least if a large volume of data is the primary aspect of the definition) and there was nothing new about it. Later in the interviews, however, most admitted that the lack of structure of much contemporary data presents both new challenges and new business opportunities.

I eventually concluded, as a result of this research, that there are real differences between conventional analytics and big data, though you wouldn't always know that from reading other books and articles about the topic, where the distinctions are often very fuzzy (see table 1-1 for a summary of the differences). I'll explain these differences, and some key similarities, later in this chapter and the rest of the book. However, I will consistently argue that big data, despite my reservations about the name of the phenomenon, is here to stay and of substantial importance

TABLE 1-1

Big data and traditional analytics

	Big data	Traditional analytics
Type of data	Unstructured formats	Formatted in rows and columns
Volume of data	100 terabytes to petabytes	Tens of terabytes or less
Flow of data	Constant flow of data	Static pool of data
Analysis methods	Machine learning	Hypothesis-based
Primary purpose	Data-based products	Internal decision support and services

to many organizations. I hope to persuade you to join me in that opinion—but don't give up your skepticism yet.

After all, if you believe that big data is important to you and your organization, you would have to do something about it. You would need to decide which aspects of it make the most sense to apply to your business and get to work on them. You'd need to hire, rent, or start to develop the kind of people who make big data work. And you'd need to change your technology architecture as well. Again, I'd feel that this book was successful if you started to do those things, but only if they make sense for you—and in any case, you would need to be convinced first.

The goal of this book, then, is not to sell you on big data, but to help you make effective decisions about it. I'll tell you what has impressed me about big data, but I will also tell you what aspects of it are oversold. I'll tell you the industries and organizations I think are going to be transformed by it, but also those that aren't likely to be affected much, at least for a while. And if you do decide to move ahead with big data, I will tell you the most reasonable and economical ways to do so.

And while I want to be respectful of your time and managerial attention, I hope you are open to the idea of mobilizing around a big data project. It may be only an exploratory one to start building some capabilities, but I do think that most organizations should be moving in this direction. At the very least, your management team should be discussing the topic of how big data fits into your business.

It's probably better to start with my assumptions about who you are as a reader. I'll then explain some of my reservations about big data, which relate to the name and the level of faddishness around the topic. Then, in the remainder of this chapter, I will tell you why I think big data is a big deal.

Who Are You?

Who are you to be interested in learning about the business implications and value of big data? I have some assumptions about who you are (although perhaps you found this book lying on an airplane seat or clicked on the wrong book as a Kindle download!). The readers of my previous books on analytics have typically been smart, ambitious businesspeople who believe in the ability of data and technology to change the rules of business. I suspect you have the same characteristics.

Specifically, however, I've found that the executives most interested in big data come from data-intensive functions like marketing, supply chain, and, increasingly, finance and human resources. Executives whose functions support big data, such as those in IT, are also often quite interested in learning more about the concept. Particularly interested executives work in industries that are either already highly data oriented, such as online businesses, or those that have the potential to be reshaped—potentially any industry, but particularly those with a lot of consumer data—such as retail, travel and transportation, telecommunications, media and entertainment, and financial services.

Finally, if you're a student preparing for a career—or at least a job or two—in big data, congratulate yourself on your perspicacity. This field is likely to be booming for many years.

If you're like most of the managers and professionals I come across, you are certainly aware of the term *big data* and know that data has been growing at an amazing rate. But you may be a little fuzzy on what is actually different about big data and how it relates to traditional data management and analytics. More importantly, most of your organizations aren't doing much with it yet. In a 2013 survey of almost one thousand *Harvard Business Review* readers, for example, many respondents said they were familiar with the concept of big data, but only 28 percent said that their organizations were "currently using big data to make better business decisions or create new business opportunities." Only 23 percent said their organizations had a strategy for big data. Only a small percentage, 6 percent, strongly agreed that "My organization has considered the impact of big data on key functions within the business," and an even smaller percentage, 3.5 percent, strongly agreed that, "My organization knows how to apply big data to our business."

That's probably why you turned to this book—to help your organization address such questions, and perhaps to benefit your own career in doing so. I'd like to think that you came to the right place!

Deconstructing the Term *Big Data*

As with many of the executives with whom I have discussed this phenomenon, I like everything about the *big data* concept except for the name itself. The concept, as I have already hinted, is revolutionary and holds transformational possibilities for almost every business. The term itself, however, is a problematic one, for a variety of reasons.

First, there is the issue that *big* is only one aspect of what's distinctive about new forms of data, and for many organizations, it's not the most important characteristic. A 2012 survey by NewVantage Partners of over fifty executives in large organizations suggests that for large companies, addressing the lack of structure of data is more salient than addressing its size. In that survey, 30 percent of respondents said that the primary data issue driving them to consider big data was "analyzing data from diverse sources," another 22 percent were primarily focused on "analyzing new data types," and 12 percent were focused on "analyzing streaming data." Only 28 percent were focused on analyzing data sets of 1 terabyte or greater, and many of that number (13 percent) were oriented to data sets between 1 and 100 terabytes—not a large volume by big data standards.[3]

There are several other issues with the term as well. The term *big* is obviously relative—what's big today won't be so large tomorrow, and as the previously mentioned survey suggests, what's big to one organization is small to another. I generally think of *big* as describing a tenth of a petabyte or more, but the only real way in which "size matters" with data is in the amount of hardware you will have to buy to store and process it.

Some have defined big data in terms of the *three Vs* (volume, variety, and velocity); others have added even more Vs (veracity, value—perhaps venality is next) but this is also problematic. Granted, these are important characteristics, but what if you only have one or two of the Vs? Does it mean that you have only a third or two-fifths of big data?

One other problem is that too many people—and vendors in particular—are already using *big data* to mean any use of analytics, or in extreme cases even reporting and conventional business intelligence. It is a well-established phenomenon that vendors and consultants will take any new, hot term and apply it to their existing offerings—and that has already happened in spades with big data.

But be careful if you're reading books, articles, or ads about big data; if they refer to reporting, "data-driven decision making," or conventional analytics, you are consuming ideas that are useful and valuable, but not particularly new.

Because of these problems with the definition, I (and other experts I have consulted) predict a relatively short life span for this unfortunate term. It was embraced by the media and by start-ups, but I have already observed that technology-oriented people in big companies—particularly those that have had large volumes of data for many years, like banks and transportation companies—are reluctant to embrace the term. As I'll describe further in chapter 8, they feel that the current generation of new data sources and types is but one of many previous new generations. Of course, that doesn't mean the "phenomenon previously known as big data" will go away. If you want to describe the broad range of new and massive data types that have appeared over the last decade or so, I know of no better umbrella term than *big data*.

However, because the term is so imprecise, organizations need to deconstruct it a bit in order to refine their strategies and signal to stakeholders what they are really interested in doing with these new types of data, and which types are most important. There are, of course, many variations on big data to choose from—it's a veritable Chinese menu of possibilities, as table 1-2 shows. You can start by choosing one from each column.

TABLE 1-2

A menu of big data possibilities

Style of data	Source of data	Industry affected	Function affected
Large volume	Online	Financial services	Marketing
Unstructured	Video	Health care	Supply chain
Continuous flow	Sensor	Manufacturing	Human resources
Multiple formats	Genomic	Travel/transport	Finance

In other words, instead of saying, "We're embarking on a big data initiative," it's probably more constructive to say, "We're going to analyze video data at our ATMs and branches to better understand customer relationships." Or if you're in health care, you could decide to "combine electronic medical records and genomic data to create personalized treatment regimens for patients." In addition to clarity about your intentions and strategies, this approach avoids endless discussions about whether the data involved is big or small (in fact, few organizations confess to working with "small data," even though it's a perfectly respectable activity—and I was taught that for a term to be truly useful, its opposite also needs to be valid).

Of course, you can use a fashionable term to your advantage as well. If your organization is one that responds only to new and shiny management objects—and if big data is still relatively new and shiny at the time you are reading this—by all means embark upon a big data project, or BDP. In other words, if calling it big data works to mobilize energy and enthusiasm in your firm, go for it. However, be ready to "pivot" (speaking of fashionable terms!) to the next new fashionable term for these activities when it appears; IBM already has a research center for "Massive Data"—surely "Gargantuan" or "Humongous" data can't be far behind!

In this book I will continue to use the term *big data* because there is currently nothing else that describes the collection of attributes in question. But I'm convinced that deriving real value from this messily named resource derives from going several levels deeper into it.

Is Big Data Here to Stay?

Perhaps we can agree that big data has an unfortunate name. But is it here to stay, or simply a fad? Is it the Hula-Hoop or pet rock of the information management world? If so, business leaders can safely ignore it. But if big data is an important and long-term feature of the business environment, then organizations and managers ignore it at their peril.

There are certainly faddish elements to the big data idea, particularly since the broader notion behind it is not particularly new. The idea of analyzing data to make sense of what's happening in our businesses has been with us for a long time (in corporations since at least 1954, when UPS started an analytics group), so why do we keep having to come up with new names to describe it? The general activity of making sense of data has been called *decision support, executive support, online analytical processing, business intelligence, analytics,* and now *big data* (see table 1-3).[4] There are certainly some new elements in each generation of terminology, but I'm not sure that things have evolved enough to be worthy of six generations.

TABLE 1-3

Terminology for using and analyzing data

Term	Time frame	Specific meaning
Decision support	1970–1985	Use of data analysis to support decision making
Executive support	1980–1990	Focus on data analysis for decisions by senior executives
Online analytical processing (OLAP)	1990–2000	Software for analyzing multidimensional data tables
Business intelligence	1989–2005	Tools to support data-driven decisions, with emphasis on reporting
Analytics	2005–2010	Focus on statistical and mathematical analysis for decisions
Big data	2010–present	Focus on very large, unstructured, fast-moving data

What makes big data somewhat worthy of a new term are the new and more voluminous forms of data that it involves—2.5 quintillion (that's 2.5 followed by eighteen zeros) bytes per day generated around the world, by one estimate.[5] Less structured data types, as I've suggested, are even more worthy of a new term and approach. Some data types, like text and voice, have been with us for a very long time, but their volume on the internet and in other digital forms herald a new era, as do the new technologies that allow analysis of such data. Social media data are truly new, from Facebook and Pinterest pages to tweets. I don't know if all of these data forms will remain; the normal pattern is for the functions performed by these tools to be incorporated into broader applications. The data generated by them and the insights they reveal about their authors, however, are not going away.

In general, however, *sensor data* is here to stay. The number of networked devices overtook the global population of humans in 2011. Analysts estimate that fifty billion sensors will be connected to the internet by 2025 ("the Internet of Things"), and each one can produce a passel of data. While early prognostications suggested that internet-connected sensors would primarily be used in consumer devices, there has been only limited progress in that regard. Our refrigerators may not be connected to the internet anytime soon (if they were, they could, for example, automatically order fresh milk to be delivered when we run low), but our TVs, security systems, and thermostats are increasingly networked. Each such device generates data that can be managed to optimize usage, consumption, and provision of services.

Sensors are also being attached to animate objects like cows and people. Roger Parks, the chief information officer of agriculture and livestock firm J.R. Simplot, for example, has taken to describing something he calls the "digital cow." The company is experimenting with embedding sensors in cow stomachs (cows have four stomach compartments, and for some reason the second stomach appears to be the optimal location) to measure temperature. If the cow is sick, the sensor will let a veterinarian know there is a problem while there is still time to treat the disease. Other researchers are experimenting with sensors that would detect the presence of *E. coli* bacteria in cow stomachs. With all these sensors, let's hope there is still room for feed in the cow's stomach!

Human beings are also being increasingly "sensored" (a word I have just coined), typically for reasons of health and fitness. We're in the age of *auto-analytics*, or the capturing and analysis of personal fitness, productivity, and health data.[6] The earliest popular application of personal analytics I know of was the Nike+/iPod combination released in 2006. The Nike+ shoe, when connected to an iPod, could capture and display running time and distance, pace, and calories burned. Since then, Nike and Apple have proliferated a variety of means to capture data on your exercise (heart rate sensors, cardio fitness equipment links, clothing with sensors incorporated, etc.), and the many Nike+ users (reportedly over five million) often upload their data to their laptops and to the Nike+ website. You can monitor your running trends, challenge friends, and get online coaching for training programs.

Since 2006, a lot of other personal analytics sensor programs have proliferated. Like Nike+, many deal with sports. Garmin Connect, for example, allows athletes of various stripes to log their activities, plan new routes, and share their exploits with others. Zed9 tracks social fitness, CycleOps tracks your bicycling power, Concept2 tracks your rowing workouts.

But increasingly personal analytics are going beyond sports into the realms of health, wealth, work, and life satisfaction in general. Withings introduced the WiFi- and Twitter-connected scale and seems to be moving into blood pressure and other connected health devices. A variety of providers, including MyZeo, WakeMate, BodyMedia, and Fitbit, offer sleep analytics (my Fitbit recently informed me that I had 97 percent sleep efficiency—I was ecstatic!). Now Me-trics, a Michigan-based start-up, is offering a general tool for measuring and monitoring personal analytics in virtually any realm of life, including health, mood, finance, fitness, online activity, and so forth. The day I logged onto the Me-trics site, Marie was tracking intimate encounters (now I've got your attention!) and Ryan was tracking water consumption. No doubt there will soon be custom-built sensors for metrics like these.

If that weren't enough data on human activity, smartphones are with us almost all the time and record our locations, conversations, and, increasingly, our purchases. Computers can keep track of virtually every aspect of our lives at work, as Stephen Wolfram, the CEO of Wolfram Research, has illustrated in his own work.[7] He knows, for example, exactly when he sent each of the third of a million e-mails he has sent since 1989. Sensors also track our pets. Perhaps our moods and brain waves will be captured and analyzed soon as well.

The bulk of data from sensors, however, may eventually come from "the industrial internet"—a very large number of networked devices in plants, transportation networks, energy grids, and so forth. GE considers this development to be potentially revolutionary in terms of both data volumes and potential benefits. It estimates, for example, that gas blade monitoring in energy-producing turbines alone can produce 588 gigabytes a day—seven times the volume of Twitter data produced in a day.

If these voluminous sources of big data aren't enough to get people motivated to embrace it, software vendors are also providing a push—or perhaps their customers are pushing them. They may sometimes pour old wine into new big data bottles, but overall there has been a sea change in the nature of business software. We are moving beyond automating transactions to analyzing the data they generate. When SAP generates more money from business intelligence and analytics than from its transactional suite of applications, a major transition has taken place. When firms like HP, EMC, and Oracle make major acquisitions and product announcements in the big data and analytics space, something new is going on. When IBM has spent close to $20 billion on analytics-related acquisitions, it's a permanently changed ball game. Even Microsoft—the company founded to support small data on personal computers—has made several product announcements involving big data. I'll have more to say about big data technologies later on in this book (primarily in chapter 5). At this point, however, I'd just like you to agree that with so many large vendors lining up behind big data, the concept is unlikely to go away.

More data, more technology—what else is necessary to ensure that big data is no flash in the pan? As I will argue throughout this book, it's the *people* who really make big data work. The role of *data scientist*, which I'll discuss at some length in chapter 4, is to my mind the primary gating factor in whether big data succeeds within an organization. The data is often free or cheap, the hardware and software are free or inexpensive, but the people are expensive and difficult to hire. I'll say much more in chapter 4 about why this is such a difficult problem, but my point here is that it's going to get much easier. Many universities offer business intelligence or analytics degree programs or concentrations, and a good proportion are adding big data topics and skills to their curricula. A number of big data and data science programs are currently being developed at schools. It won't be long before universities are churning out qualified students by the tens of thousands. This will make it much easier to undertake big data projects within companies and will prevent a labor shortage from choking off the big data movement.

All of these supply factors suggest that big data and its associated concepts and technologies are hardly fads, but will be with us for many decades. For these ideas not to matter, businesses and organizations would have to stop caring about how to save money, sell more products and services, and delight customers. None of that seems likely to happen.

What's New from a Management Perspective?

I'll describe what's new about big data technology in chapter 5. But as is normally the case, while technology issues can be challenging, the more difficult issues involve management and people topics. Some of them are so new that there are hardly any answers to them yet. For others, there are already glimmers of solutions.

I've already mentioned one of these issues, which is getting the right kinds of people to do big data work. I can't emphasize enough that people are the key to making this work. While there is nothing entirely new about needing people for analytical activity, the kinds of people needed to do big data initiatives—the data scientists—are definitely different from conventional analysts. They are more facile with data, more experimental, and more product-focused. I'll have much more to say about them in chapter 4.

Since the data, technology, and people are all somewhat different from those employed in traditional analytics, there is a need for some new organizational structures to accommodate big data. You can't simply assume that big data goes into the IT organization. In large organizations, big data groups can be found in marketing, finance, product development, strategy, and IT. I'll have more to say in chapter 3 about where they fit best under different circumstances.

Traditional information management and analytics were primarily about supporting internal decisions. Big data is somewhat different in this regard. Granted, there are many cases when it is used for that purpose, particularly in large organizations. But instead of creating reports or presentations that advise senior executives on internal decisions, data scientists commonly work on customer-facing products and services. This is particularly true in big data start-ups, but it's also the case in larger, more established companies. For example, Reid Hoffman, the cofounder and chairman of LinkedIn, made his data scientists a line product team for the company, and they have developed such products as People You May Know, Groups You May Like, Jobs You May Be Interested In, Who's Viewed My Profile, and several others. GE is primarily focused on big data for improving services and is already using data science to optimize the service contracts and maintenance intervals for industrial products. Google, of course—the ultimate big data firm—uses data scientists to refine its core search and ad-serving algorithms. Zynga uses data scientists to target games and game-related products to customers. Netflix created the well-known Netflix Prize for the data science team that could optimize the company's movie recommendations for customers. The testing firm Kaplan uses its data scientists to begin advising customers on effective learning and test-preparation strategies. These companies' big data efforts are directly focused on products, services, and customers. This has important implications, of course, for the organizational locus of big data and the processes and pace of new product development.

For those uses of big data that do involve internal decisions, new management approaches are still necessary, but not yet fully resolved in practice. This is because big data just keeps on flowing. In traditional decision support situations, an analyst takes a pool of data, sets it aside for analysis, comes up with a model, and advises the decision maker on the results. However, with big data, the data resembles not so much a pool as an ongoing, fast-flowing stream. Therefore, a more continuous approach to sampling, analyzing, and acting on data is necessary.

This is particularly at issue for applications involving ongoing monitoring of data, as in social media sentiment analysis. *Sentiment analysis* allows an organization to assess whether the comments about its brands and products in blogs, tweets, and Facebook pages are positive or negative on balance. One potential problem with such monitoring applications is the tendency for managers to view a continuing stream of analysis and reports without making any decisions or taking any action. "Sentiment is up . . . no, it's down . . . hooray, it's back up again!" For ongoing monitoring work, there should be processes for determining when specific decisions and actions are necessary—when, for example, data values fall outside certain limits. Such information helps to determine decision stakeholders, decision processes, and the criteria and timeframes for which decisions need to be made.

Even the United Nations—an organization typically not known for its agility—is getting in on this new approach to deciding. The UN's Global Pulse innovation lab has developed a big data-related tool called HunchWorks, which is clearly a monitoring-oriented application of big data. The lab describes HunchWorks as "the world's first social network for hypothesis formation, evidence collection, and collective decision-making."[8] The idea is that as data begin to reveal a trend or finding—say, for example, weather data suggesting a drought that could lead to famine in a part of Africa—an analyst would post the hunch and the data on which it was based, and others could weigh in with new analyses and data. Such suggestive hypotheses have been described as "digital smoke signals."[9] One goal is to determine how likely the hunch is to be worthy of detailed analysis and action. But the idea that the UN would have a system for circulating data-driven hunches marks a major change in that organization's culture.

Whether the analysis and decision processes are social or individual, the continuing stream of big data suggests that organizations need to think about new ways of making decisions with this resource. If it's worth investing in the collection and analysis of big data, it's also worth thinking about how the outcome of the analysis will have an impact on decisions and actions.

New Management Orientations from Big Data

Big data changes not only technology and management processes, but also basic orientations and cultures within organizations. We simply can't think about business in the same way with this new resource.

One needed change in orientation is toward more discovery and experimentation with data.[10] To date, a primary focus of business and technology organizations has been to stably automate processes such as marketing, sales, and service. Analytics has been used to understand and tune the processes, keeping management informed and alerting them to anomalies ("exception reporting" has been a key aspect of business intelligence). Business and technology architecture often reflect this flow, starting with transactions and operations and moving—one hopes—to analysis and insight. Companies review performance, plan improvements, and implement them through technology projects that span months and years.

Big data flips this approach on its head. The basic tenet is that the world—and the data that describes it—are in a constant state of change and flux, and those organizations that can recognize and react quickly and intelligently have the upper hand. The prized business and IT capabilities are discovery and agility rather than stability. Data scientists working with big data tools and technologies will be able to continuously mine new and existing data sources for patterns, events, and opportunities at an unprecedented scale and pace.

This new orientation is relatively straightforward for small start-ups, and indeed it is often found in the ones I have researched and describe in chapter 7. However, it requires a sea change in IT attitudes and activities within large organizations. It is typical to hear that 75 to 80 percent of an analyst's time is spent sourcing, cleaning, and preparing data for analysis. This is true in both companies and government organizations. Carey Schwartz, leader of the Pentagon's "Data to Decisions" strategic initiative, believes that, without dramatic improvements, data volumes from next-generation sensors and the complexity of integrated systems will far outpace the ability of analysts to consume it.[11]

The Pentagon and Schwartz are right to worry about this issue. Like many private-sector firms, the military is accumulating data at a rate faster than it can analyze it. For example, the drone aircraft favored by the US military of late not only shoot missiles at terrorists but also capture video data of the territory over which they fly. The video data could be very useful to military forces, but only if it is analyzed. And apparently there are not enough human analysts to deal with all the video data. In 2012, Secretary of the Air Force Michael Donley lamented that it will take years for Air Force analysts to analyze all the video data that the drones capture. Apparently, the Air Force is working on approaches to analyzing the data with less human intervention.[12]

At the Pentagon, Schwartz is looking to big data technology to make analysts (video and otherwise) a hundred times more productive. He emphasizes the need for "analytics that work," which he describes as analytics that are reliable and robust and capable of being automated. The analytics, algorithms, and user interfaces must be connected to provide new methods to interact with and support the "human in the loop." Perhaps some of this push toward automation is being driven by the fact that at least one "human in the loop" in the intelligence community, Edward Snowden, used the data from the military and intelligence machinery to become what Michael Hayden, a former CIA and National Security Agency director, called "the most costly leaker of American secrets in the history of the Republic."[13]

One element of the new architecture for big data is the view of discovery and analysis as the first order of business. Data scientists (as well as general business analysts) need continuous access to an analytics platform or *sandbox* (a term that captures the discovery-oriented mission for big data) that supports ready insight to enterprise and external data. The platform needs to facilitate integrating new data, ad hoc queries, and visualization to accelerate human understanding. As valuable insights emerge from this platform, they become the requirements for changes to production systems and processes.

Companies also need to adopt new methodologies for insight and data-based product development. Traditional waterfall—highly structured approaches that only yield a result at the end of a long process—methods have been increasingly forced out of system development processes in favor of faster and more flexible *agile* processes. Agile approaches, in which relatively little time is spent specifying a system up front and more emphasis is placed on creating small deliverables quickly, can also apply to analytics and big data. Imprecise, slow requirements gathering for a new analytical system or process is replaced by iterative experimentation, insight, and validation.

Of course, not all IT is discovery; the greatest value of an insight is typically derived by using it in production processes and systems. Once an insight has been extracted from data, it needs to be classified—as irrelevant to the business, interesting but not useful, or the basis for an action. Similarly, if the big data analysis has led to a new product or feature, it needs to be adopted or dropped or considered for adoption at a later date.

The UN HunchWorks example mentioned previously also illustrates another aspect of big data that needs to change management orientations. HunchWorks is also described as "a mechanism to make the membranes between silos of knowledge both inside and outside of the UN more permeable." An important aspect of big data is that it is often external to the organization using it. Whether one is addressing internet data, human genome data, social media data, the Internet of Things, or some other source, chances are good that it doesn't come from your company's internal transaction systems. The exceptions to this pattern—which I'll describe in chapter 2—are most likely to be in the telecommunications and financial services industries, which are blessed with massive amounts of internally generated data to analyze. Even there, however, internal data can often be profitably supplemented with external data.

This marks a major change in the orientation of companies. Peter Drucker commented in 1998 that most information systems were focused on internal accounting data and "have aggravated what all along has been management's degenerative tendency, especially in the big corporations: to focus inward on costs and efforts, rather than outward on opportunities, changes, and threats . . . The more inside information top management gets, the more it will need to balance it with outside information—and that does not exist yet."[14]

Now, with big data, the external focus is beginning to exist. As one big data start-up executive (Christopher Ahlberg, CEO of Recorded Future) said, "It seems to me that we have squeezed all the juice out of the internal information. Maybe it's time we focused on the whole world of external information."[15] I'd argue that there is still some juice to be extracted from internal sources, but there is certainly more information outside of organizations than within them.

For external data to become embedded into decisions, products, and services, many managers will have to change their mind-sets and habits. They'll have to regularly survey external sources of data to see what might be available and how it might support their organization. They'll simply have to turn their gaze outward—to suppliers and their suppliers, to customers and their customers, and to business and political risks. And, as I have just suggested, they'll have to develop systematic criteria to help them decide and act when the external information is viewed as significant.

The New Opportunities from Big Data

Of course, if big data is to make substantial inroads into businesses, it must provide some new opportunities. Going on about how much data there is in Facebook or Twitter, or the number of gigabytes in a single human genome, doesn't help executives determine how much value they will achieve from exploiting big data.

There are three classes of value: cost reductions, decision improvements, and improvements in products and services. I'll describe the cost-reduction opportunities from big data technology later in this book; suffice it to say here that they are potentially quite substantial. On the decision side, the primary value from big data derives from adding new sources of data to explanatory and predictive models. Many big data enthusiasts argue that there is more value from adding new sources of data to a model than to refining the model itself. For example, Anand Rajaram, who works at @WalMartLabs and teaches at Stanford, ran a bit of a natural experiment in one of his Stanford classes along the lines of the Netflix Prize—the contest that invited anyone to try to improve the Netflix customer video preference algorithm and win a million bucks.[16] One of the groups in Rajaram's classes used the data that Netflix provided and applied very sophisticated algorithms to it. Another group supplemented the data (illegally, according to the rules of the competition) with movie genre data from the Internet Movie Database. The latter group's predictions were far more successful. Rajaram also attributes much of Google's success over earlier search engines to its use of additional hyperlink data.

As Peter Norvig, Google's director of research, puts it: "We don't have better algorithms. We just have more data."[17]

In real organizations as well, decisions of various types can be improved by adding big data. If you have some data predicting customer attrition based on what customers have or haven't bought from you, you can probably improve it by adding data from these customers' service transaction histories. If you have a model that predicts the "next best offer" that individual customers are likely to buy based on their purchase history and demographics, you can probably improve it by analyzing some of the customers' comments and likes on social media sites. Some of the extra data you may use will be "big" in that it's large-volume or unstructured, but some will be small and/or structured. The key is to look broadly for new sources of data to help make your decision.

The other major new opportunity from big data is to create appealing products and services for customers. I've already mentioned that this benefit was not one that I often encountered when discussing conventional business intelligence and analytics. It's still early days for big data in general and for data-based products and services specifically, but there are many examples of desirable products and services deriving from big data. I'll talk about more of these in chapter 2, but citing a few here may give you an idea of the potential benefits.

I've mentioned the role of big data and data-based products at LinkedIn, but one specific offering that has definitely provided value to that company is the People You May Know (PYMK) feature. As many readers will know from having used it, PYMK suggests to LinkedIn members (customers) some other members that they may want to connect with. PYMK employs a multifactor approach to identify possible new connections, including shared schools, workplaces, connections, and geographies. Many people, including me, find it somewhat uncanny in its ability to identify long-forgotten relationships.

More importantly for this context, PYMK has generated a lot of new customers for LinkedIn. Compared with the other prompts LinkedIn sent to get people to come back to the site, PYMK messages achieved 30 percent more click-throughs. Millions of people paid repeat visits who would not have done so otherwise. Thanks to this one feature, LinkedIn's growth trajectory shifted significantly upward. Another factor attesting to the value of the PYMK feature is that many other social sites—including Facebook, Twitter, and Google+—have added similar capabilities, although I think LinkedIn's is still the most effective.

For another example, the online travel systems company Amadeus has developed a big data service offering called Featured Results. Faced with a business challenge of rising importance—the fast-increasing "look to book" ratio, or the number of online queries per airline ticket booking—Amadeus needed some way for travel distributors to make desirable offers to customers. Based on databases of user queries, "several hundreds of millions" of live airline prices, and half-a-billion reservation records, Featured Results presents four possible itineraries in which customers may be particularly interested. Early results of a beta test with Vayama, a travel agency partner of Amadeus, suggests that Vayama has found a 16 percent improvement in its ratio of sales to searches.

Many executives may admit that big data has the potential to add substantial value to online businesses, but are less sure of the value outside of that domain. They might be persuaded of the relevance of this resource to them by the actions and plans of GE—one of the world's largest and most successful companies and one of the most enthusiastic adopters of big data—even in industrial businesses.

GE has set up a center in the San Francisco Bay area to address software and big data issues and is hiring lots of data scientists to do so. They will work on GE's traditionally data-intensive businesses, such as financial services and health care. But here I want to discuss some of the potential value that GE sees in industrial applications, such as in the company's locomotive, jet engine, and gas turbine businesses. GE sometimes refers to devices in industries like these as "things that spin," and it expects that most, if not all, of them will soon be able to capture and communicate data about their spinning.

One such spinning device is the gas turbine, which GE's customers use for energy generation. GE already monitors more than fifteen hundred turbines from a centralized facility, so much of the infrastructure is in place for using big data to improve performance. The company estimates that it could get at least a 1 percent improvement in efficiency of monitored turbines from software and network optimization, better dispatching of service, and improved gas/power system harmonization. This may not sound like much, but it would amount to $66 billion in fuel savings over the next fifteen years.

GE makes a lot of its money these days on servicing industrial products, so if it had proprietary data on how these products are performing and when they might break down, it could promise customers more effective operations and optimize the cost and effectiveness of service operations. Imagine that you were buying a turbine for a power plant. You have the choice of one with big data output, continuous performance monitoring, and optimized service only when it's needed. The other turbine doesn't have those features. Which would you buy, and which might you be willing to pay a bit extra for?

GE is also thinking that big data–based optimization of service operations will work well for many of its other big-ticket industrial goods, including locomotives, jet engines, and medical imaging machines. Of course, other companies in those industries could adopt the same approaches, and they probably will someday. But GE's scale, ambitious investment plans, and early start in the big data area will probably confer considerable competitive advantage.

What We Don't Know—and Won't for a While

It's not yet clear whether giant firms like GE will be the primary beneficiaries of big data and how other firms will respond. Just as we don't know what the industry and competitive dynamics will be for big data–enabled industrial products and services with GE and its competitors, there are many other uncertainties about big data that we will have to live with for a good while. It's worth thinking about these issues now, however, because you want to have a planned response to them rather than an accidental one.

We don't know, for example, how big data will affect organizational structures. There is reason to believe that the availability of big data—on operations, employees, customers, and business risks—will benefit those organizations that centralize their capabilities to capture and analyze the data. We already see this with small data analytics; many organizations have begun to build centrally coordinated analytical strategies and groups. If big data resides in silos and pockets across organizations, it will be very difficult to pull it together to understand and act on business opportunities. However, because big data is so new, we don't really know what form the organizational transformations around it will take. The early results from big companies, which I review in chapter 8, suggest that big data will be combined with existing data and analytics groups, but that could change over the next few years.

We also don't know how big data will affect customer relationships. The overall direction that big data enables is more knowledge of customer behaviors, likes, and dislikes and more targeting of ads, products, and services based on that knowledge. However, there is already evidence that customers don't want more targeting—and that they are deeply suspicious of what companies do with their data. Sixty-eight percent of American internet users, for example, say they disapprove of targeted ads based on their search and website histories.[18] Despite these theoretical objections, Americans often seem willing to give up a substantial amount of personal information in exchange for either social interaction (as on Facebook, for example) or discounts on merchandise. However, at some point there may well be a substantial backlash in the United States—regulatory or in terms of customer behavior—to targeting based on big data. There already has been a strong regulatory push in the European Union to restrict companies' exploitation of customer data. I don't see anything imminent on the US regulatory horizon, but organizations should certainly carefully monitor customer sentiment—and the possibility of stepping over the "creepiness factor" limits of customers—in this regard.

We also don't know how big data will change management. Big data gives us the opportunity to move toward a greater degree of data-driven decisions. Companies and organizations will increasingly know more about their business environments, and they'll be able to use analytics—both automated and in support of human decisions—to decide and act on what they know. It's not yet clear at what pace managers will adopt these new approaches. But history would indicate that it's unlikely. After all, small data analytics have been around for decades, yet many managers still make gut-based decisions—and power and politics certainly are unlikely to disappear from organizations anytime soon. And while my friends Erik Brynjolfsson and Andy McAfee talk and write often about the decline in importance of the "Hippo"—the highest-paid person's opinion—such animals are hardly extinct in the organizations I visit (though it would certainly be desirable if this transpired quickly).[19] If you count on the disappearance of power and politics from decision making, you are likely to be disappointed—at least in the short run. It's probably safe to plan on more data-driven management in the future, but the exact trajectory of the adoption is unclear, and will vary widely across organizations.

What's Coming in This Book

The final word for this chapter is that we know the opportunities and impact of big data will be substantial, but we don't yet know the details of how companies and industries will be affected. Now, let's preview the content of the forthcoming chapters (you might want to skip around if some issues are more interesting to you than others).

In chapter 2, I'll describe what people and companies are beginning to do with big data in key industries and functions—and what they might do in the near future in several scenarios—which may provide some greater clarity on the transformational nature of this new resource.

Chapter 3 addresses the idea of a strategy for big data—how your organization can decide what business objectives it wants to achieve with this resource, whether you should pursue data discovery versus production applications, and how rapidly to move on big data opportunities.

Chapter 4 addresses one of the major constraints to success with big data—the human factor. It describes just what skills a data scientist needs and also discusses the emerging topic of how big data will change management behaviors.

If you're hearing a lot of talk about "Hadoop" and "MapReduce" and you're having a tough time making sense of this jargon, you may want to turn directly to chapter 5, which is a manager-focused guide to big data technology. It treats not only these infrastructural technologies for managing big data, but also some of the analytical approaches useful in the big data environment, such as machine learning and visual analytics.

Chapter 6 takes a broad perspective to the topic of what organizations need—beyond smart people and new technology—to succeed with big data. If you read my coauthored book *Analytics at Work*, you'll be familiar with the DELTA model, which I apply to big data in the chapter. (I also use the model, with a slight modification, in a big data capability assessment framework in the appendix.)

The last two chapters address what big data means for different sizes and ages of organizations. Chapter 7 focuses on the learning we can extract from start-ups and online firms, while chapter 8 focuses on what large, established companies are doing with big data. In chapter 8, I advance an idea I call "Analytics 3.0," which describes how companies can combine the best of small data and traditional analytics with the big data approach.

In exchange for the effort of reading all these chapters, you'll get a comprehensive understanding of how big data can be put to work for you and your organization. At the end of each chapter, I will list some action-oriented questions that you and your management team should be asking and answering in order to harness this powerful resource. Throughout the book, there's not a lot of gee-whiz talk about how wonderful this vast amount of data is, but rather a perspective on how it can be put to use. Remember—as I suggested at the beginning of this chapter, it's not how much data you have, but what you do with it that counts.

How Important Is Big Data to You and Your Organization?

- Has your management team considered some of the new types of data that may affect your business and industry, both now and in the next several years?

- Have you discussed the term *big data* and whether it's a good description of what your organization is doing with data and analytics?

- Are you beginning to change your decision-making processes toward a more continuous approach driven by the continuous availability of data?

- Has your organization adopted faster and more agile approaches to analyzing and acting on important data and analyses?

- Are you beginning to focus more on external information about your business and market environments?

- Have you made a big bet on big data?

How Big Data Will Change Your Job, Your Company, and Your Industry

Big data is such a broad business resource that it is sometimes difficult to envision all the ways that it can affect an organization and an industry. Therefore, I'll start this chapter by describing several future scenarios for how big data might yield a transformational impact on a company or industry. It's also likely to change the nature of work for many individual job roles, as the scenarios illustrate. Although each of the technologies needed to execute on these scenarios is actually available today, I suspect it will take several years for organizations to implement them. The challenges are more in the nature of systems integration—developing data standards and pulling the necessary data together—and business change, rather than pure technology.

If you enjoy speculation about the future, you'll probably like these scenarios. If you are a hardnosed resident of the present, skim these ideas about the future quickly and get to my assessment of the role of big data in key industries and business functions. In each of these sections, my goal is to persuade you that big things are coming from big data and that you should start thinking now about how to react.

As a general rule, I am pretty confident that big data is going to reshape a lot of different businesses and industries. For example, here are a few industry categories that might be transformed in a substantial fashion:

- Every industry that moves things

- Every industry that sells to consumers

- Every industry that employs machinery

- Every industry that sells or uses content

- Every industry that provides service

- Every industry that has physical facilities

- Every industry that involves money

I haven't done a systematic classification, but I suspect that this list encompasses every industry! The more detailed scenarios and industry/function analyses in the remainder of this chapter should provide some backup for this sweeping argument.

Four Future Scenarios

In this section, I'll describe four future scenarios for how big data will be used in several different industries in the future. They may seem far-fetched, but many of the big data innovations that make them possible are already in existence today.

A Big Data Scenario for Business Travel

Lynda Peters, an IT architect at insurance firm Tranquilife, is going to a business conference in March 2016; the subject is "Truly Massive Data and Its Impact on Insurance." It is a popular topic, and she was almost denied the permission to attend because the employee activity system at Tranquilife revealed that six other employees had already registered. Fortunately, she was able to convince her boss that she really needed to go.

After Lynda registers for the conference, all the logistics—city, hotel, beginning and ending times—are automatically downloaded into her scheduling application. They are then transmitted—again automatically—to the travel management system that Tranquilife had chosen. The travel management system links to the agenda and details for the conference, and swings into action on her behalf. Without any actions on Lynda's part, she receives a proposed itinerary with the following components:

- A flight on her preferred airline, with a frequent flyer upgrade already arranged and her preferred aisle seat reserved

- A hotel reservation for all the nights of the conference

- A self-driving rental car reservation at the airport (because the conference hotel is forty miles away, and the travel management application has compared the cost at prevailing rates of taxi, limo, and rental car for that distance)

- A reservation at the best Italian restaurant in the conference city—Lynda's favorite dining option—for the "on your own" night of the conference, with three suggestions (and three alternate suggestions) for dining companions who are valued members of her social network and who will also be attending the conference; Lynda needs only to touch her tablet screen once to invite them

Lynda's self-driving car delivers her to the conference hotel with no problems; the travel management system had downloaded her destination address, preferred air-conditioning temperature, and favorite satellite music station to the car. Lynda's only complaint about self-driving rental cars is that antiquated regulations force her to sit in the driver's seat, which limits her tablet access. She also resents the laws that prevent her from watching movies and TV while the car drives her; soon, she expects, these would be relaxed.

On the way to the conference, Lynda notes on her tablet that the organizers have recommended some excellent sessions based on her learning preferences and records in her business network profile of past sessions she'd attended. Also, she notes that one invited member of her dinner party will be unable to attend the conference, so her travel management app is now recommending an invitation to the first alternate.

Lynda enjoys the conference, and even before she leaves, she notes that the data on sessions she attended (confirmed by her smartphone's location certification app) have been added to both her business network profile and Tranquilife's HR database. A couple of the sessions have even given her a little boost in her salary. After she returns to work, she receives an e-mail from the travel management system noting that all of her travel expenses—even an estimate of her hotel tips—have been submitted to her company for reimbursement. The automatically transcribed text and presentation slides from all conference presentations that Lynda highlighted as relevant to her company—along with her annotations—have been posted in the personal portals of all employees who showed an interest in massive data. Her notes suggest that insurance will never be the same after massive data, and neither will the experience of traveling to learn about the coming changes.

(*Note to skeptics:* Although many of these automated travel features are not yet available, travel management experts I interviewed suggested that they would be plausible in the fairly near future. And we know that the self-driving car already exists—described by Google as a big data project—and will probably be incorporated into the transportation system in some fashion.)

A Big Data Scenario for Energy Management

David Byron is a corporate facilities and energy manager for Bathworks, a large US plumbing fixtures manufacturing company. He is in charge of facilities and energy management for Bathworks's twenty office campuses and facilities around the country. He and his firm have a strong desire to save energy and use all possible tools and behaviors to do so, while keeping employees comfortable and company assets safe.

One key aspect of Bathworks's energy management involves its fleet of vehicles. All company vehicles, including company cars (some driver-managed, some automated), are on a wireless network. As a result, at any time Byron knows their locations, distances traveled that day or overall, average and peak speeds, and acceleration and braking patterns. Drivers who operate vehicles in such a way as to waste energy or to put the driver and vehicle at risk are sent reminder e-mails and text messages. Some employees have found this monitoring invasive and turned down company cars. Most, however—including all senior executives—have become accommodated to it.

Byron and his staff also closely monitor and control energy consumption of the Bathworks's heating, ventilation, and air-conditioning (HVAC) systems. They know the temperature, humidity, light levels, and human presence in every room of every building—over twenty-three thousand spaces are monitored. From the central climate management center, temperature can be instantly raised or lowered, and windows and shades opened or shut. They can tell if an office, floor, or building is currently occupied, or if a damper in an airflow passage is broken. They have predictive models of the best time to raise summer temperatures in a building, and the optimal time to turn on the heat on winter mornings. This micro-controlled climate environment has already saved Bathworks more than 20 percent in three years on its HVAC-related energy use.

Byron has also implemented the ability to remotely control energy access to a number of inessential devices in order to lower consumption at particularly expensive times of the day and year. Copiers, printers, and even vending machines can have their energy reduced if needed. The company also provides onsite charging for electric vehicles, and charging rates can also be dialed down during energy shortages or expensive supply periods.

Byron's team has integrated all of these diverse systems into a Facilities Data Operations Center in a nondescript building behind the headquarters location. It looks like the *Starship Enterprise* holodeck, but there is seldom a need for the energy management equivalents of Captain Kirk and Mr. Spock; most of the systems are fully automated. Byron likes to explain to visitors that the company has laid an "analytical blanket" on top of the diverse systems used to manage the buildings.

Byron is beginning to look at some other frontiers in energy management, but they involve substantial investment in generation technologies. He has a plan to install solar and wind energy generation devices on many of the Bathworks's buildings and is working with vendors to shape an RFP. The performance of these devices could be optimized based on the amount of available wind or sunlight, time of day, and price of energy. Byron knows this is a good idea, but unlike its other big data energy management tools, which have been done fairly inexpensively, Bathworks will need to spend considerable money to save money on energy generation.

(*Note to skeptics:* After dreaming up this futuristic scenario, I read that it's not that different from what leading firms are already doing. Microsoft, in particular, has published an account of how it does similar activities on its own campus. In fact, the term *analytical blanket* comes from that document.[1])

A Big Data Scenario for Video Analytics for Retail

Latitia Harris is a senior marketing executive for Pettopia, a pet products and services chain with over 220 stores in North America. Harris has been concerned for many years that Pettopia might be at a disadvantage in competing with online pet products retailers, which can know each of their customers' identities and what they have bought and shopped for. Pettopia has a loyalty program, but many customers don't belong to it, and the company can identify some customers only via their credit cards. There is also a small but significant shoplifting issue in the stores, in that customers often give treats to their pets from the treat bar without paying for them.

Harris concludes that video analytics are the key to solving all these problems and will thus give Pettopia competitive parity or even advantage with online firms. Therefore, she introduces video cameras into each store and begins a program of video analytics. These analytics are necessary because there is far more video content than any human viewers can digest, and Harris is interested in fast response for some applications.

One of the first applications that Pettopia develops is a simple store visitor counter, so that Harris can compare visitors to sales and compute the level of conversions. That information is used to understand which employees are best at converting customers and to adjust staffing levels at different times. It takes only a small extension to this system to analyze how often employees offer help to customers who seem to be looking for something in the store.

However, that's only the beginning. The next application is more complex, and involves actually identifying the customers and even pets coming into the store. Based on matches of video images with loyalty cards, credit cards, check information, and the pet name inquiries at checkout, Pettopia is able to identify 90 percent of customers and 60 percent of pets. Harris learns that while customers find it somewhat creepy if store personnel knew their names without being told, they are delighted to have their pets recognized. So names of both customers and pets are displayed on mobile devices as soon as they came into the store.

Harris has also sponsored the development of an application that notes what products customers have looked at—but didn't buy—on a trip to the store. If they have an e-mail address for the customer, they can send an e-mail offering that product at a discount on the next visit or through an online order, and this move has resulted in a high conversion rate. Pettopia has also been able to bring in some additional revenue by selling information to manufacturers about which customers spend time at the manufacturer's endcap display.

The most recent use of the video analytics system involves the shoplifting from the treat bar. Pettopia's video system is able to determine how many treats were taken from the bar, and to display the number at the register when the customer (and pet) arrive at checkout. For small numbers of treats taken by frequent customers, checkout personnel are instructed not to say anything on the first shoplifting occasion, and to say only "Your dog seems to really enjoy those treats" on the second. On any subsequent occasions, or if the customer is not loyal to Pettopia, the checkout employee simply announces, "Plus four treats from the treat bar, correct?" and adds the price to the total. Some customers have been surprised, but treat revenues have increased by 5 percent from the program.

Harris has been experimenting with other video analytics applications, including one that indicates whether pets need grooming, and another offering training program discounts for poorly behaved pets based on analysis of their behaviors in the store. She feels that she is only scratching the surface of what can be done with the big data analytics from video content.

(*Note to skeptics:* Video analytics are becoming increasingly capable, and could probably already perform most of the tasks described in this scenario if trained to do so.[2] I know that facial recognition of humans is quite far along already; facial recognition of dogs may be a few years off, but would seem to be possible.)

A Big Data Scenario for Home Education

Larry DiCecco is a seventeen-year-old high school junior. His parents know that he has a lot of raw intelligence, but his grades haven't been terribly impressive, and they feel that he hasn't exerted himself in school. They very much want him to go to college, and are concerned that unless he makes some additional effort, he won't get into the college of his choice. Larry's parents are not well off, and know that he will have to get considerable financial aid to afford college. Based on his results on the preliminary SAT college admissions exam, they also know that he needs tutoring to improve his college testing outcomes, but they can't afford to pay a human tutor.

The parents have heard from the school's guidance counselor about an "AutoTutor" program from a test preparation company. They research the program and decide to subscribe to it for several months. It is much less expensive than paying a human tutor. All of the test prep content is supplied in digital form, and Larry's consumption of the content is "instrumented" so that the AutoTutor program can monitor his study habits.

After beginning the AutoTutor service, Larry and his parents quickly discover that his study habits are ineffective. The system has detected, for example, that Larry falls asleep too often, employs too much highlighting, and generally studies too slowly because he does too much rereading (which suggests that he isn't concentrating while he studies). To no one in the family's surprise, the program suggests that Larry has been multitasking while he studies—texting his friends, checking Facebook, listening to his favorite Pandora station, and occasionally playing a video game. He now makes a sincere effort to stop at least some of these activities while studying.

The program analyzes his vocabulary and determines that he is weak on science-related terms, so it offers drills involving those types of words. In math, it diagnoses that he has strong algebra skills but is weak on geometry, and it thus gives him a series of targeted geometry exercises.

There is a writing component of the SAT test, and the AutoTutor service has promised to improve Larry's writing skills—at least those that are tested. The program has him write a series of essays, and automatically grades them. It finds that Larry's essays are weakest in terms of the topic sentences in each paragraph, and offers him a set of drills to strengthen this skill.

After each session on the computer or tablet, the score improvement app calculates Larry's predicted SAT score range and the most likely percentile for each section of the test. He begins to make steady improvement in his predicted score.

The app also gets Larry's parents involved in the learning and improvement process, sending them advice about Larry's behaviors and progress, and recommending motivational interventions they might undertake that are targeted to Larry's situation and the program's inferences about his attitudes and behaviors. After some discussion with his parents, Larry actually seems to be making some progress in his schoolwork as well.

Larry uses the AutoTutor service steadily for two months for far less money than a human tutor would have cost. The test preparation company has no human contact with Larry, but the family is very satisfied with the outcome. Larry improves his SAT score by 150 points (at the midpoint of the AutoTutor's predicted range), and gets into his first-choice college. He only wishes he could keep using AutoTutor to improve his grades once he enrolls there.

(*Note to skeptics:* Companies like Kaplan, Capella, and the University of Phoenix are already doing some of what is described in this scenario. Large online education consortia such as Coursera and edX are also pursuing research on the feasibility of such measurement and recommendations. The area of big data from education will, I predict, be a major focus over the next several years, and what Larry does in this scenario will probably become commonplace.)

Making These Scenarios Real

These (I hope) provocative scenarios, or others like them, could become real in your business and industry. Raw technological capabilities are unlikely to be the barrier to them—in fact, as my notes to skeptics suggest, most aspects of the scenarios are possible today, at least on an experimental or pilot basis. What is needed most is the vision and determination of organizations to build and deploy these innovations. Considerable imagination, courage, and commitment will be required to embark on these big data journeys. Each will take a considerable amount of data collection, IT development, systems and data integration, and analytical model development, and firms could use some help with new and more productive tools for such activity. The scenarios will require a number of smart people to work for several years to make them possible. In some cases, they will require regulatory change (e.g., to allow self-driving cars on the nation's highways).

It's not entirely clear what the viable business model for each of these innovations is—how companies can make money with them. It's also not clear that customers will want these innovations—particularly those like the pet store video cameras that pose a risk to human and pet privacy. However, it seems likely that some organizations will pull them off, and that they will make those organizations very successful. Just as Google, for example, decided to make the self-driving car a reality, there are other organizations that will succeed with integrating it into a comprehensive travel management capability. Would you rather have your company be the architect and creator of these scenarios or a competitor?

Industries Well Suited to Big Data

In my previous research, I found that, with regard to traditional structured data analytics, some industries were definitely ahead of others in the race to understand their businesses and customer relationships (see table 2-1). The leaders—I call them *overachievers*—tended to be those in consumer-oriented industries with a lot of data to process: credit card companies like Capital One, insurance firms like Progressive, consumer travel companies like airlines and hotels, and casino companies like Harrah's (now Caesars). Some consumer products companies, like Procter & Gamble, became good at analytics even without direct consumer data. When internet companies emerged in the mid-1990s, the smart ones like Amazon, eBay, and Netflix quickly

TABLE 2-1

Historical industry use of data and analytics

Data disadvantaged	Underachievers	Overachievers
Health-care organizations	Traditional banks	Consumer products
B2B firms	Telecom	Insurance
Industrial products	Media and entertainment	Online
	Retail	Travel and transport
	Electric utilities	Credit cards

became leaders in analytics because there was a large amount of data to crunch—and they did so well. I referred to them in my *Competing on Analytics* research as "analytical competitors from birth."

Data disadvantaged organizations were those that didn't have much data—or if they did, their data wasn't well structured. They were analytically impaired for this reason. These organizations included:

- Health-care providers, which were disadvantaged because they didn't yet have widespread electronic medical records and also had a lot of text-based notes about patients (50 percent of electronic medical record data consists of unstructured text)

- Business-to-business (B2B) firms, which were disadvantaged simply because they didn't have very many customers—and hence couldn't really do much with customer data

- Business-to-business-to-consumer (B2B2C) firms, which had intermediaries between them and their consumers (for example, retailers between consumer products firms and consumers, or doctors between pharmaceutical companies and their consumers), and hence often couldn't get good data about who was buying their products and how they were being used

- Industrial products firms, which often fell into the disadvantaged B2B category and didn't have much data about their products

Other industries had more data, but were simply *underachievers* with it—not using it effectively to benefit customers or themselves. These included:

- Telecom firms, which had lots of data, but for some reason did not take advantage of it (perhaps because they had historically been a regulated monopoly or because they were busy with mergers and acquisitions)

- Media and entertainment firms, which underachieved because they had decision cultures based on intuition and gut feel, and didn't know how to assess whether people were looking at their content or not

- Retailers had great data from point-of-sale systems, but most have underachieved with it until recently; Tesco and to some degree Walmart have been higher achievers

- Traditional banks have massive amounts of data on the money their customers consume and save, but for the most part they have been underachievers in helping those customers make sense of it all and presenting targeted marketing offers to them

- Electric utilities have been talking about the "smart grid" for a while, but are still a long way from achieving it; apart from some limited rollouts of smart metering devices and time-of-day pricing, very little thus far has happened in the United States

This environment has changed dramatically with the advent of big data. Many of the also-ran industries in the previous generation of analytics can be leaders in the big data race, although in order to do so they need to change their behaviors and attitudes. Big data will be available in their business and industry, but the laggards need to work harder to take advantage of it than they did with traditional analytics.

So let's think about what big data is likely to be available, and how it's likely to be used, in some of those industries.

Health Care

In health care, for example, there will be much more structured data from the many electronic medical record systems that hospitals and outpatient clinics are installing. In addition, there have always been voluminous amounts of text in the clinical setting, primarily from physicians' and nurses' notes. This text can increasingly be captured and classified through the use of natural language processing technology. Insurance firms have huge amounts of medical claims data, but it's not integrated with the data from health-care providers. If all of that data could be integrated, categorized, and analyzed, we'd know a lot more about patient conditions. Image data from CAT scans and MRIs is another huge source; thus far doctors only look at it but don't analyze it in any systematic fashion. Human genome data—at about 2 terabytes per human—is rapidly becoming inexpensive enough ($1,000 per patient within a few years) to gather on many patients. And if that weren't enough, there will be massive amounts of data from *connected health* (telemedicine and remote monitoring) and *quantified self* (personal monitoring) devices.[3] Imagine that doctors and hospitals could gather data on every patient's weight, blood pressure, heart rate, physical activity, and even mental state—every day or even every hour or minute! The amount of data boggles the mind. In sum, the primary challenge in the health-care industry won't be how to gather big data, but how to make use of it all.

B2B Firms

Businesses that sell only to businesses may not have a large number of customers, but they still have a big data future. One aspect of it is to consider not businesses, but the individuals that work in those businesses, as a company's real customers. Some B2B marketers are already beginning to do that, and to track movement of individuals across companies. In addition, big data can arise from capturing conversations, service calls, sales inquiries, and other aspects of the broad customer relationship. Finally, since many B2B products and services will be "instrumented" with chips and sensors that measure how they perform, companies will have a large amount of data on how their customers are actually using their products. With all this data, it's likely that B2B firms can catch up to their consumer marketing colleagues in their reliance on big data and analytics.

B2B2C Firms

The consumer-oriented firms with intermediaries between them and their customers—I mentioned consumer goods makers and pharmaceutical firms—that have been at an informational disadvantage in the past can catch up in the world of big data. Overachievers in this category, like Procter & Gamble, are venturing into online sales. P&G calls its online sales presence an "eStore," and uses it not only to sell more products, but to learn from consumers about their behaviors and preferences. P&G is also working closely with major retailers like Walmart to share and analyze the large volumes of retail point-of-sale data. Others firms with intermediaries, like GM and Ford in the automobile industry, may not have direct exposure to their customers in car sales, but they learn a lot about customers through credit card relationships. Consumer products firms are beginning to use video analytics to learn more about consumers. PepsiCo, for example, employs a "Learning Lab" from video analytics vendor RetailNext to better understand what motivates a consumer to pull a six-pack of Pepsi off the shelf. Pharmaceutical firms are likely in the future to not only sell drugs, but also devices—perhaps "smart" pillboxes or medicine cabinets— that record whether or not a drug has been taken at the prescribed frequency. While it's unlikely that pills and soda cans themselves will have built-in sensors anytime soon, there will be plenty of data to analyze.

Industrial Products Firms

The big data for industrial products firms is likely to come from sensors and chips embedded in industrial products. I've already mentioned GE's plans (and current activity) around monitoring locomotives, gas turbines, and aircraft engines. John Deere plans to gather big data from sensors and computers in its tractors. Boeing gathered a massive amount of in-flight data on its troubled 787 Dreamliner and was able to fix it faster as a result (though most of the problems with the plane's batteries seemed to happen on the ground). Cisco Systems collects data on network performance and knows which network configurations are most likely to be reliable. Intel has an application to identify that your personal computer is having problems, and needs to be fixed or replaced before it crashes. Companies like these will know the condition of the equipment they have sold, so they'll be able to service it more effectively and know when it needs to be replaced. And they're also likely to benefit from some of the B2B big data innovations mentioned previously, as well as some of the manufacturing and supply chain innovations I describe next.

Telecom Firms

Firms in the telecom industry—including internet service providers, wireline and mobile telecom services firms, and cable television firms—have had, as I noted before, lots of data on who communicates with whom, who is interested in what content, and who's willing to spend serious money on networks. Just to give you an idea of how much data, IBM estimates that there are 5.2 million gigabytes of mobile data generated each day.[4] Even the number of phones is approaching big data levels; the average household, according to Neustar, has 3.8 phone numbers.[5] Unfortunately, however, the industry just hasn't done much yet with all this data. You may have noticed that whether you are a big spender or a small spender on telecom, you are generally treated the same way as a customer. Some firms—particularly in the mobile telecom services industry—have focused on using data to identify customers who are likely to drop their service or attrite. A few of these mobile providers are beginning to analyze aspects of the social networks among their customers, and, for example, to identify particularly influential customers who might influence others in their "tribe." These companies are only scratching the surface of what might be done in this industry, however. The telecom industry is one of the few that doesn't really have to gather a lot of new data to succeed with big data; it simply needs to make use of what it already has. In chapter 8, I'll describe what Verizon Wireless is doing to create new businesses based on selling mobile data.

Media and Entertainment Firms

This industry faces a bonanza of big data opportunities. Although it hasn't done much with data or analytics in the past, the fact that the industry increasingly distributes its products over the internet means that it can now learn a huge amount about what types of content customers really want. The industry could understand not only what kinds of movies, television programs, and short videos people enjoy, but could also acquire much more granular information. What stars bring out the viewers? Are consumers more likely to consume happy or sad content? Does profanity turn off certain viewers— or keep them watching? The current "batting average" of media and entertainment companies is very low; most movies don't make money, and most television shows are quickly canceled. It doesn't have to be that way. When companies like Netflix and Amazon enter the content-creation business, they are showing a new way to use big data to design content that succeeds. Netflix knew before it launched its *House of Cards* series that the director, star actor, and British version of the same program had all done well with its audiences in the past—so doing a US version was close to a no-brainer.[6] Amazon. com launched fourteen pilot programs for its streaming video service and used customer feedback on it to help it select the five it ultimately produced. These big data–based models will surely penetrate to other content creation organizations shortly—particularly because they seem to be very effective.

Banks

The banking industry is already beginning to take advantage of the data it has on customer payments and financial activities, though there is plenty of room to grow with big data. Banking is now a multichannel activity, and some large banks are starting to understand the complex journeys customers make through call centers, branches, ATMs, and online websites to meet their financial needs. They are also beginning to customize marketing offers to customers. However, I have yet to find the bank that truly uses all of its customers' financial data to make personalized and high-quality recommendations for financial products. I hold out hope that this will come in the big data age.

Electric Utilities

The opportunities in the utilities industry are quite substantial, though companies would have to make significant investments to make them a reality. Possibilities include enterprise decisions around where to invest in new generation and distribution capabilities, grid operations involving real-time energy management decisions, and consumer intelligence about how people use energy.[7] A variety of equipment, software, and services firms are offering big data solutions for the industry, but thus far few utilities have engaged with them.

———————

Although I've described only a few industries, I hope you're getting the impression that virtually every industry can be transformed by big data. If the laggard industries in the era of traditional analytics can excel with big data, it's likely that virtually every industry can succeed with it.

Big Data and Key Business Functions

In addition to industry, the other key element of organizational structure is the business function. In this section, I'll describe the impact of big data on the key business functions of virtually every large organization. While the impact of big data on some functions is greater than others, you may not be surprised at this point to learn that I think there are major opportunities to exploit big data in all of them.

Marketing

Marketing has been the happiest home for traditional analytics, but this function still has a lot of room for improvement with big data. New sources of data for marketing purposes include customers' social, mobile, and locational data. Imagine the value of knowing not only what your customer is saying about you in social media, but exactly when he or she has entered your store. In addition to these relatively new data sources, many marketers still haven't fully harnessed online data. Most marketers today wish for "omnichannel" relationships with customers—those that let consumers move seamlessly between multiple physical and virtual touchpoints—but few have achieved that elusive goal. They need to know how customers move from one channel—say, the online one—to a call center to solve a particular problem, or to a retail store to check out the merchandise. Integrating and analyzing data—some big and unstructured, some smaller and more structured—across multiple channels is, then, the primary big data agenda for marketers. They also need to accurately attribute sales to the variety of ads and messages they have sent out through the various channels. This is a complex analytical task, but there is software to analyze it and prioritize marketing spending accordingly.[8] Of course, before marketers achieve these goals, it's likely that a new channel or two will emerge. Therefore, big data for marketing is a never-ending task.

Sales

The sales function has been transformed over the past several years with the introduction of customer relationship management and call reporting systems. Companies generally now have a much better idea of what their sales forces are doing and of the prospects in the sales pipeline. One step forward would be to begin noting how accurate salespeople's predictions of closing sales are by comparing predictions and actual sales, though this would be relatively small-volume, structured data. It would also be possible to use smartphones and car location devices to monitor how salespeople actually spend their time. While this would undoubtedly generate a lot of interesting data, it would probably be very unpopular with the sales force.

Supply Chain

Supply chain processes are among the most likely to be transformed by big data. Radio-frequency identification (RFID) devices—long discussed as a means of monitoring supply chain movements—are now actually becoming available at a reasonable cost. GPS tracking on trucks and trains means that arrival times for shipments can be more precisely predicted. Transportation companies, including UPS, FedEx, and Schneider National, have already installed tracking devices and are increasingly using them to monitor and optimize their networks. In chapter 8, I describe how UPS, for example, has recently used data from its package cars (brown trucks) to redesign its driving route structure for only the third time in over one hundred years. Other types of sensors are likely to lead to a flood of additional data and opportunities to analyze it. RFID and telematics sensors primarily track location, but so-called ILC (identification, location, condition) sensors can monitor the condition of goods in the supply chain as well, on such variables as light, temperature, tilt angle, g-forces, and whether a package has been opened. They can transfer data in real time via cellular networks. Obviously, the potential to identify supply chain problems in real time and take immediate corrective action is greatly enhanced with this technology. We have only begun to explore how analytics might be used to enhance the value of ILC-derived data.

Manufacturing

There are many opportunities to apply big data in manufacturing. Not only manufactured products but also manufacturing equipment increasingly contain data-producing sensors. Machining, welding, and robotic devices can report on their own performance and need for service. These devices are networked, so they can be monitored and controlled from a central control hub. And the prevailing trend to employ more automation in factories will continue and probably accelerate.

Manufacturing operations can also connect with big data-fueled supply chains to ensure that product supply is available to feed manufacturing, and that only the optimal amount of goods is manufactured. Discrete manufacturing companies have largely addressed this issue, but process manufacturing (oil companies, for example) have not made as much progress.

Human Resources

HR has been one of the least data-driven functions in the past, but HR information systems and analytics based on them are beginning to change that. This function could go a substantial step further in terms of analyzing employee location and communication data. For example, if we're trying to decide where to locate facilities, shouldn't we understand the locations of employees throughout their workdays before making that decision? No special sensors are necessary; mobile phones could easily supply the data if employees gave permission to harvest it. If we think it's important that certain groups collaborate with each other—for example, that product development communicates with manufacturing—shouldn't we measure the level and nature of collaboration? Server log files already allow such analytics, but very few organizations use them. The best organizations of the future will be those that design and actively monitor the collaborative and communication activities of their people. Alex (Sandy) Pentland, an MIT professor, has analyzed these types of human behaviors using the sensor trails they leave behind, and believes they are an invaluable guide to redesigning organizations and societies.[9]

Strategy

The strategy function, often charged with making or supporting some of the most important decisions within an organization, has historically been rather bereft of data in analyzing those decisions.

Strategists may have gathered some data—or hired an external strategy consulting firm to do so—but it was rarely voluminous. Now, not to use a large amount of external data in strategic decisions might actually become strategic malpractice. The big data that is probably most relevant to such big decisions is internet data—addressing what people around the world are saying and doing. Three start-up firms that support this type of analysis are Quid, based in San Francisco; Recorded Future, based in Boston; and Signals Intelligence Group, based in Israel. Quid analyzes internet data to understand the prevalence of and connections between technology-related content. For example, it analyzed technology opportunities for a large IT vendor, and found that there were unexplored opportunities at the intersection of biopharma, social media, gaming, and ad targeting. Recorded Future analyzes internet data to understand predictions and temporal events; it is used by government intelligence agencies and by companies such as Procter & Gamble, which uses its data and tools to understand what events might affect sales forecasts. Signals uses principles from the Israeli military organization to inform strategists about innovation, competition, supplier relationships, and product development at consumer products firms like P&G, pharmaceutical firms such as Novartis and Johnson & Johnson, and technology firms.[10] In short, if you are simply relying on internal information and your own experience, you are going to come up short as a strategist.

Finance

The financial services industry was perhaps the first to adopt big data. Financial traders and risk managers chewed through vast amounts of data to identify buying or selling opportunities, or to assess the likelihood that investments and assets would crater in value. Although the financial crisis of 2008–2009 revealed that these analyses were sometimes unreliable, these uses of big data continue apace. Analyses based on it will identify patterns in rising and falling assets and can also be used to identify customer marketing opportunities, as well as to detect fraud and money laundering. It is likely that in the near future, big data will find its way into corporate finance departments as well (though in the early days of big data, corporate finance has been something of an underachiever). These organizations also do trading, risk management, hedging, and other data-intensive activities. With the greater availability of external data, they are likely to become more involved in assessing the risk of working with particular customers, suppliers, and business partners.

Information Technology

The IT function, which often stores and crunches big data, could also rely much more on data in making its own decisions. Two areas that could use more data-based decisions are the reliability and security of IT operations. Virtually all IT devices—computers, network equipment, storage devices—throw off data about their own performance that can be analyzed, explained, and predicted. Neither IT organizations nor their vendors have used much of this data to optimize the reliability and performance of their operations, but there is an opportunity to do so. The availability of IT capabilities in "the cloud" will accelerate this trend, as cloud services vendors will need to document and improve their reliability to get and keep customers. Security is another IT domain where more analytics are needed. Instead of simply responding to security breaches, organizations need to predict where and from whom security threats will emerge. What are the attributes that predict someone will try to hack into a system? What have been the most vulnerable areas in the past? Those organizations that can anticipate—and stop—security threats will inevitably be more successful than organizations that merely plug holes when they become obvious.

Summary of Big Data's Impact

I've provided some future scenarios and some ideas about how big data might transform key industries and functions. But many opportunities still fall between these cracks. How about the analytics of traffic, crime, and water management in local government? What will big data do to agriculture—the oldest industry, but one that is increasingly creating a lot of data? What happens when our homes—our thermostats, refrigerators, and home theater systems—become smart, digitized, and connected to the internet? How will big data analytics—derived from player locations or video footage—transform sports? It's impossible to foresee all the impacts of big data.

The key point is not to be complacent. I recently talked with a senior R&D executive at a large automobile manufacturer. We were discussing big data, and I mentioned the Google self-driving car as a big data project of enormous impact in his industry. I then asked whether his own company had a similar project. "We're leaving that one to Google," he said.

That's probably a big mistake. If big data is going to transform your industry, shouldn't your company be involved in the transformation—and not just a victim of it? That sort of complacency has doomed many a company to failure. To get out ahead with big data, you need to have extended discussions within your company about what this new tool might mean for your industry and business, and about what your response should be. To do nothing is to put your job and your organization at great peril.

ACTION PLAN FOR MANAGERS

How Will Big Data Change *Your* Organization?

- Have you envisioned any future scenarios for how big data might change your industry, business models, and customer experiences?

- Is it anyone's job today to monitor and inform senior executives of developments in big data that relate to your business?

- Have you considered the impact of big data on the key functions within your business?

- Does your senior executive team have regular discussions about the role of big data and analytics within your business?

- Have you converted any of this thinking and discussion into action?

3

Developing a Big Data Strategy

Let's say that you are intrigued by the possibility of big data and want to begin capitalizing on its potential for your business and industry. What do you do first? Buy a big Hadoop cluster for your data center? Hire a bunch of data scientists? Copy all the internet data ever created and store it in your data center?

Hold on! First, you need to do some thinking about where big data fits into your business. There will be plenty of time to pursue the other tactical steps I've mentioned, important as they are. But the most important step is to decide on a particular strategy for big data. You need to assemble your senior management team and start talking about what big data can do for your company and which of its many possibilities you want to pursue. That process should start with some serious thinking about the objectives you want big data to fulfill.

What's Your Big Data Objective?

Like many new information technologies, big data can bring about dramatic cost reductions, substantial improvements in the time required to perform a computing task, or new product and service offerings. Like traditional analytics, it can also support internal business decisions. Which of these benefits are you seeking? The technologies and concepts behind big data allow organizations to achieve a variety of objectives, but you need to focus a bit—at least at first. Deciding what your organization wants from big data is a critical decision that has implications for not only the outcome and financial benefits from big data, but also the process—who leads the initiative, where it fits within your organization, and how you manage the project.

Cost Reduction from Big Data Technologies

If you're primarily seeking cost reduction, you're probably conscious of the fact that MIPS (millions of instructions per second—how fast a computer system crunches data) and terabyte storage for structured data are now most cheaply delivered through big data technologies like Hadoop clusters (Hadoop is a unified storage and processing environment for big data across multiple servers; see chapter 5 for a more detailed explanation). One company's cost comparison, for example, estimated that the cost of storing 1 terabyte for a year was $37,000 for a traditional relational database, $5,000 for a data appliance, and only $2,000 for a Hadoop cluster—and the latter had the highest speed of processing data under most circumstances. I'll provide some other figures in chapter 8, and they also show substantial savings.

Of course, these comparisons are not entirely fair, in that the more traditional technologies may be somewhat more reliable, secure, and easily managed. And in order to implement a new Hadoop cluster and all its associated tools, you may need to hire some expensive engineers and data scientists. One retailer, GameStop, decided not to pursue work with Hadoop because it didn't want to train its engineers in the software or bring in consultants for help with it.[1] But if those attributes don't matter—perhaps you already have the necessary people, for example, and the application doesn't need much security—a Hadoop-based approach to big data could be a great bargain for your company.

If you're focusing primarily on cost reduction, then the decision to adopt big data tools is relatively straightforward. It should be made primarily by the IT organization on largely technical and economic criteria. Just make sure that they take a broad perspective on the cost issues, pursuing a total cost of ownership approach. You may also want to involve some of your users and sponsors in debating the data management advantages and disadvantages of this kind of storage, but that's about it. No detailed discussions about the future of your industry are necessary.

Cost reduction is the primary objective for one large US bank, for example. The bank is actually known for its experimentation with new technologies, but like many such institutions these days, it's become a bit more conservative. The bank's current strategy is to execute well at lower cost, so its big data plans need to fit into that strategy. The bank has several objectives for big data, but the primary one is to exploit "a vast increase in computing power on dollar-for-dollar basis." The bank bought a Hadoop cluster with fifty server nodes and eight hundred processor cores that is capable of handling a petabyte of data. It estimates an order of magnitude in savings over a traditional data warehouse. Its data scientists—though most were hired before that title became popular—are busy taking existing analytical procedures and converting them into the Hive scripting language to run on the Hadoop cluster. According to the manager of the project:

> This was the right thing to focus on, given our current situation. Unstructured data in financial services is sparse anyway, so we are doing a better job with structured data. In the near to medium term, most of our effort is focused on practical matters—those where it's easy to determine ROI—driven by the state of technology and expense pressures in our business. We need to self-fund our big data projects in the near term. There is a constant drumbeat of "We are not doing 'build it and they will come'"; we are working with existing businesses, building models faster, and doing it less expensively. This approach is less invigorating intellectually, but more sustainable. We hope we will generate more value over time and be given more freedom to explore more interesting things down the road.[2]

If your situation is like the bank's, you may want to focus primarily on cost reduction as well. Keeping a laser-like focus on that objective—and not being seduced by the other blandishments of big data—will help to ensure that it is achieved.

Cost reduction can also be a secondary objective after others have been achieved. Let's say, for example, that your first goal was to innovate with new products and services from big data. After accomplishing that objective, you may want to examine how to do it less expensively. That was the case, for example, at GroupM, the media-buying subsidiary of the advertising conglomerate WPP.[3] The company buys more media than any other organization in the world, and it uses big data tools to keep track of who's watching it on what screen. This would be fine, except that GroupM has 120 offices around the world, and each office has been taking its own approach—with its own technology—to big data analytics. If the organization allowed each office to implement its own big data tools, it would cost at least $1 million per site.

Instead of this highly decentralized approach, GroupM plans to offer centralized big data services out of its New York office. It will focus on twenty-five global markets and expects that it will spend just over a third of the amount per site that the decentralized approach would have required. We will probably see many more such consolidations in the next several years as firms that allowed decentralized experimentation with big data attempt to rein in their costs.

Time Reduction from Big Data

The second common objective of big data tools is reduction of the time necessary to carry out particular processes. Macy's merchandise pricing optimization application provides a classic example of reducing the cycle time for complex and large-scale analytical calculations from hours or even days to minutes or seconds. The department store chain has been able to reduce the time to optimize pricing of its 73 million items for sale from over twenty-seven hours to just over one hour. Software vendor SAS has named this application *high-performance analytics* (HPA). HPA obviously makes it possible for Macy's to reprice items much more frequently to adapt to changing conditions in the retail marketplace. Theoretically, the retailer could reprice according to daily weather conditions, for example (although electronic tagging would make this much easier!).

This HPA application takes data out of a Hadoop cluster and puts it into other parallel computing and in-memory software architectures. Macy's also says it has achieved 70 percent hardware cost reductions. Kerem Tomak, vice president of analytics at Macys.com, is using similar approaches to time reduction for marketing offers to Macy's customers. He notes that the company can run a lot more models with this time savings: "Generating hundreds of thousands of models on granular data versus only ten, twenty, or one hundred that we used to be able to run on aggregate data is really the key difference between what we can do now and what we will be able to do with high-performance computing."[4] Tomak also makes use of visual analytics tools for his big data results, which is common with big data.

A financial asset management company provides another example. In the past, research analysts there could analyze a single bond issued by a city or company, and do risk analysis based on twenty-five variables, with perhaps one hundred different statistical simulations of model results. It's a much better analysis to use one hundred variables and a million simulations. That was impossible three years ago, but now such a fine-grained analysis—a couple of trillion calculations—can be done in ten minutes on a big data appliance.

As the chief information officer described the benefit of this approach, "The primary advantage is that the discovery process becomes very fast. An analyst can build models, run them, observe what happens, and if he doesn't like something, change it, all in one minute. This cycle used to take eight hours—if you could do it at all. The train of thought is much more continuous, which means a higher quality of research."[5]

If your company is primarily interested in time reduction, you need to work much more closely with the owner of the relevant business process. A key question is, what are you going to do with all the time saved in the process? Respectable business-oriented answers include:

- We're going to be able to run a lot more models and better understand the drivers of our performance in key areas.

- We're going to iterate and tune the model much more frequently to get a better solution.

- We're going to use many more variables and more data to compute a real-time offer for our customers.

- We're going to be able to respond much more rapidly to contingencies in our environment.

Bad answers (at least in strict business terms) include playing more golf, drinking more coffee, or finally having enough time for that three-martini lunch.

Developing New Offerings

To my mind, the most ambitious thing an organization can do with big data is to employ it in developing new product and service offerings based on data. One of the best at this is LinkedIn, which has used big data and data scientists to develop a broad array of product offerings and features. These offerings have brought millions of new customers to LinkedIn, and have helped retain them as well.

Another strong contender for the best at developing products and services based on big data is Google. This company, of course, uses big data to refine its core search and ad-serving algorithms. Google is constantly developing new products and services that have big data algorithms for search or ad placement at the core, including Gmail, Google+, Google Apps, and others. As I mentioned in the travel simulation in chapter 2, Google even describes the self-driving car as a big data application.[6] Some of these product developments pay off, and some are discontinued, but there is no more prolific creator of such offerings than Google.

There are many other examples of this phenomenon in both online and primarily offline businesses. GE is mainly focused on big data for improving services—among other things, to optimize the service contracts and maintenance intervals for industrial products. The real estate site Zillow created the Zestimate home price estimate, as well as rental cost Zestimates and a national home value index. Netflix created the Netflix Prize for the data science team that could optimize the company's movie recommendations for customers and, as I noted in chapter 2, is now using big data to help in the creation of proprietary content. The testing firm Kaplan uses its big data to begin advising customers on effective learning and test-preparation strategies. Novartis focuses on big data—the health-care industry calls it *informatics*—to develop new drugs. Its CEO, Joe Jimenez, commented in an interview, "If you think about the amounts of data that are now available, bioinformatics capability is becoming very important, as is the ability to mine that data and really understand, for example, the specific mutations that are leading to certain types of cancers."[7] These companies' big data efforts are directly focused on products, services, and customers.

This has important implications, of course, for the organizational locus of big data and the processes and pace of new product development. If an organization is serious about product and service generation with big data, it will need to create a platform for doing so—a set of tools, technologies, and people who are good at big data manipulation and the creation of new offerings based on it. There should probably also be some process for testing these new products on a small scale before releasing them to customers. Obviously, anyone desiring to create big data–based products and services needs to be working closely with the product development team, and perhaps marketing as well. These projects should probably be sponsored by a business leader rather than a technician or data scientist.

Taking a product/service innovation focus with big data also has implications for the financial evaluation of your efforts. Product development is generally viewed as an investment rather than a savings opportunity. With this focus, you may not save a lot of money or time, but you may well add some big numbers to your company's top line.

Supporting Internal Business Decisions

The primary purpose behind traditional small data analytics was to support internal business decisions. What offers should you present to a customer? Which customers are most likely to stop being customers soon? How much inventory should we hold in the warehouse? How should we price our products?

These types of decisions are still relevant to big data when there are new, less-structured data sources that can be applied to the decision. For example, United Healthcare, a large health insurance company, is focused on the customer satisfaction and attrition issue. Many companies have used small data analytics to measure and analyze this important factor, but a lot of the data about how customers feel is unstructured—in particular, sitting in recorded voice files from customer calls to call centers. The level of customer satisfaction is increasingly important to health insurers because it is being monitored by state and federal government groups and published by organizations such as Consumers Union. In the past, that valuable data from calls couldn't be analyzed.

Now, however, United is turning it into text and then analyzing it with natural language processing software (a way to extract meaning from text). The analysis process can identify—though it's not easy, given the vagaries of the English language—customers who use terms suggesting strong dissatisfaction. The insurer can then make some sort of intervention—perhaps a call exploring the source of the dissatisfaction. The decision is the same as in the past—how to identify a dissatisfied customer—but the tools are different.

Three major financial services firms I know of—Wells Fargo, Bank of America, and Discover—are also using big data to understand aspects of the customer relationship that they couldn't previously get at. In that industry—as well as several others, including retail—the big challenge is to understand multichannel customer relationships. They are using customer "journeys" through the tangle of websites, call centers, tellers, and other branch personnel to better understand the paths that customers follow through the organization, and how those paths affect attrition or the purchase of particular financial services.

The data sources on multichannel customer journeys are unstructured or semistructured. They include website clicks, transaction records, bankers' notes, and voice recordings from call centers. The volumes are quite large—12 billion rows of data for one of the banks. The firms are beginning to understand common journeys, describing them with segment names, ensuring that the customer interactions are high quality, and correlating journeys with customer opportunities and problems. It's a complex set of problems and decisions to analyze, but the potential payoff is high—half a billion dollars is the estimate at one of the banks.

Business decisions using big data can also involve other traditional areas for analytics, such as supply chains, risk management, or pricing. The factor that makes these big, rather than small, data problems is the use of large volumes of external data to improve the analysis. In supply chain decisions, for example, companies are increasingly using external data to measure and monitor supply chain risks. External sources of supplier data can furnish information on suppliers' technical capabilities, financial health, quality management, delivery reliability, weather and political risk, market reputation, and commercial practices. The most advanced firms are monitoring not only their own suppliers but their suppliers' suppliers.

In monitoring other forms of risk, firms can monitor big data sources on the internet. I've already mentioned the internet big data firm Recorded Future, for example. Its intelligence agency customers monitor people (known terrorism suspects), events (demonstrations or riots), and predictions (of government unrest). Its commercial customers in the corporate security function monitor protests or political unrest, and customers in the marketing function monitor competitive activity and events or predictions that might affect demand.

Competitive and market intelligence used to be a rather intuitive exercise, but big data is beginning to change that approach. If you can get more detailed data and do more systematic analysis on it, the activity will probably improve your strategic decisions. As Joey Fitts, CEO of Matters Corp., explains, "Historically, market and industry intelligence consisted primarily of company directories indicating who companies *are*—basic information such as their physical location, phone numbers, SIC code, credit score, etc., but now we can explain what organizations *do* in the market. Market factors which were hidden are now visible data, enabling trend analysis, benchmarking, segmentation, modeling, and recommendations. It's a much broader set of data, at significantly greater scale, and more real-time. Companies can lead rather than react."[8]

For example, a leading software provider sought to better understand the landscape of partner support for competitive software platforms versus their own offerings. The company leveraged Fitts' firm, Matters Corp., which monitors market activities in that industry, to untangle the web of unstructured data on partnerships and platform support. The data revealed that the competition was garnering as much as three times the partner attention and platform support. In customer terms, this meant that a much richer ecosystem of partner services—technology advisory services, assessments, implementation, applications, solutions, technology extensions and support—was available to customers of the competition than they could offer to their own customers. This recognition resulted in the company leadership proposing $100 million in additional budget to close the competitive partner gap. The company was able to use the same tools to monitor their relative impact on partner capacity and watch the gap close over time.

Pricing was an early area of business to which analytics was applied, and it was very successful. Almost every airline and hotel chain, for example, now uses pricing optimization tools to determine the best price for a seat or room. Pricing optimization was originally done with internal structured data on what goods historically sold at what price, and that's still a key element. But pricing software companies such as PROS now often incorporate external, and somewhat less structured, data into the algorithm. For example, a PROS user in the oil industry can incorporate weather data (which would influence consumer demand) and competitor prices, which can often be scraped from the internet, into pricing algorithms.

Discovery versus Production

There are two primary activities relative to big data analysis, based roughly on the stage of development involved. One is *discovery*, or learning what's in your data and how it might be used to benefit the organization. The other is *production*.

Discovery

Data discovery has long been a feature of conventional analytics, but the management challenges and business opportunities big data affords make this a particularly important activity. Discovery requires different skills, organizations, tools, financial orientation, and cultural attributes than production-oriented work with big data.

Discovery is most often done in business units rather than IT organizations, typically by people who are focused on innovation, product development, and research. Some companies organize them into "data labs" or "analytics sandboxes" or a group with a similar name.

They are typically found within the most data-intensive business units of their organizations—for example, the online or distribution channels functions within banks or marketing functions in retail and consumer products. They know the latest tools, know how to construct and monitor experiments with data, and aren't averse to failing. The classic view of a data scientist is someone who fits this profile.

This culture of learning and openness to failure—necessary in all innovators—may be difficult for some organizations to foster, but they must learn to do so. They also need to establish a budget for discovery efforts that may not show immediate or measurable returns. Though companies should tolerate failure and experimentation, this does not mean that they should allow people in data labs to work on whatever they want. As Tom Redman, a former Bell Labs data analyst, argues, the organizational and cultural focus of a data lab should be similar to what Bell Labs fostered several decades ago:

- The secret to success at Bell Labs is working half-days. And the best thing about the Labs is you can work those twelve hours any time you want.

- The secret to success at Bell Labs is having great ideas. You only need one every couple of years. But it has to improve phone service. And it has to be truly great.

- The secret to being a great manager at Bell Labs is hiring the right people, giving them the tools they need, pointing them in the right direction, and staying out of their way.[9]

The outcome of data discovery is an idea—a notion of a new product, service, or feature, or a hypothesis (with supporting evidence) that an existing model can be improved. There will be more of the incremental improvements than the grand breakthroughs; most discoveries are relatively minor. One might find a new factor to better identify customers who are about to leave you, or better target an offer. If you keep at it and have good people and a supportive culture, you'll eventually find something big.

Production

The *production* stage for big data applications is just that—putting the application into production processes at scale. It might mean merging new data and scoring approaches into a pricing algorithm, or moving a new product feature from beta release to a full-featured offering. It requires scale, reliability, security, and all those pesky attributes that customers, partners, and regulators care about.

Of course, not all discovery ideas should go into production. Not all ideas fit an organization's culture or processes or have a clear payoff. If you're sending even half of your discovery projects into production, you're probably being a bit too liberal.

Things can also go astray if not enough discovery projects go into production. For example, I recently conducted interviews at a health-care organization that has done a large number of discovery projects involving big data, including capturing and analyzing physicians' notes, radiology images, patient behaviors, and so forth. Many of these projects held considerable potential. However, the organization's electronic medical record (EMR) system, while being well suited to capturing transaction data, had limited capabilities to export data for analysis. Each attempt to do so involved large amounts of time, money, and frustration. As a result, the discovery projects seldom made it into production at all. This organization knew it had a problem in the discovery/ production handoff. It had invested a lot in its EMR system, but it hadn't yet marshaled the resources and time to create an enterprise warehouse for clinical data.

There are also important human capabilities in production of big data applications. The types of people who do production work are not entirely different from those who do discovery—they should still have some understanding of analytics—but otherwise there is a different skill mix. They should be experts at integrating new applications and hardware/software capabilities into an existing architecture and at optimizing performance of applications. They are most likely to be found in IT functions rather than business units. They must be oriented to issues of data management and governance and system reliability. Obviously, companies don't want to change production applications every day—or install new features that don't work—so some sort of testing and release management is necessary. This sort of data due diligence tends to slow things down, and the discovery people tend to be frustrated by that. At least some deliberate behavior is justified, however; in the production stage, you don't want to release an application that's still full of bugs.

And of course production is not just an IT issue. If you have a new way of making a decision in a key business process, there will also be human and organizational change issues. If you're changing pricing algorithms, for example, you have to get the sales force comfortable with them. If you're supplying some new algorithms for inventory optimization, you have to make sure that the warehouse managers actually use them. UPS, which is improving its route optimization decisions, found that the data and analytics issues were relatively easy compared with introducing the new approaches to its many thousands of drivers.

Designing Your Big Data Initiative Portfolio

In short, chapter 2 and this one should have persuaded you that there are a lot of things you can do with big data. Most large organizations should probably be doing more than one thing with it.

But how do you design a specific portfolio of initiatives? Do you work on externally facing products or internal decisions? Do you seek cost reduction, time reduction, the development of data-based products and services, or the enhancement of existing decision processes? In these benefit areas, are you at the discovery stage or the production stage? Or is big data so potentially important that you should work with it along multiple fronts at once?

These questions stem from the earlier sections of this chapter. Together, they form a matrix of objectives and stages of big data applications (figure 3-1). Each objective can be addressed through the discovery or production stages. For example, if your goal is to use big data technologies to reduce costs, the discovery activities might involve a small pilot or proof-of-concept to understand whether a Hadoop cluster or related technologies might save your company some money. Since you know that saving money is the objective, you will probably want to do a total cost of ownership (TCO) study that would include the human costs of programming and architecting the big data environment. Assuming that study has a positive outcome, you would then proceed to a full rollout of the Hadoop cluster for some production applications.

Let's take another example—a more ambitious one. Let's say you want to reinvent, or at least substantially improve, some products and services with big data. Of course, you need to decide whether products or services make more sense, and which specific ones might be a generator of big data. GE, for example, has focused on "things that spin"—turbines and locomotive engines, for example—as generators of service data. Since GE makes most of its money on services, focusing on improving service processes and operations was a pretty easy decision. It's fair to say that GE is still primarily in discovery mode in this regard and is assembling the people and infrastructure to make it happen. However, the company is already collecting lots of data from sensors and is probably not far from going into production for big data–based services.

GE has already begun to offer its "Industrial Internet" software and analysis platform to other firms, and has even developed new big data marketing labels: "Predicity" and "Datalandia." As you can imagine, this is all a pretty expensive proposition, which is why GE is investing a couple of billion dollars on it all.

The cells of figure 3-1 are not mutually exclusive, although organizations should probably focus a bit in the early days of big data—and discovery will generally precede production, of course. GE, for example, is also exploring cost and time reductions with big data technology, although the primary focus of the company's initiative is on service innovations in industrial products.

Another company that has a multipronged initiative is Amadeus, a leading distributor of travel information. Amadeus executives argue—with facts on their side—that they were into big data before big data was big. The company's data center in Erding, Germany, manages more than 370 million travel transactions a day and processes about 2.5 million bookings a day. At any given time, there are about 56 million passenger name records active within its system.[10]

As travel becomes both more democratized and more complex, customers need increasing amounts of help in navigating through the options. So a major focus of Amadeus's big data efforts involves easing the search process and presenting customers with targeted travel options—in

FIGURE 3-1

Objectives and stages for big data

	Discovery	Production
Cost savings		
Faster decisions		
Better decisions		
Product/service innovation		

other words, product/service innovation. I've already mentioned the Featured Results offering, and Amadeus is working on others as well.

In addition to this use of big data for product/service innovation, Amadeus is also working on other cells in the matrix. The company's IT organization has been implementing big data technologies—nonrelational databases, open-source data management tools, and distributed commodity server architectures—for several years with an eye toward both cost-reduction opportunities and minimizing response time for customers. The average response time to an Amadeus query is about 300 milliseconds, and IT architects would like to keep it that quick in a bigger data future. Finally, Amadeus is working with its customers to use big data for better decision outcomes. It works with airlines, for example, on how to optimize their websites through testing of different versions, and what customer preferences are for booking channels, kiosks versus human agents at airports, baggage check-in times, and many other issues. In addition to the passenger and flight records in its own systems, the company collects data on fifty other aspects of the travel domain and combines the different data types for greater decision effectiveness.

Who's Involved in What?

As I've suggested, the different types of big data objectives and project phases involve different roles and skills. In figure 3-2, I've taken the objective/stage matrix and inserted likely responsible parties for each of the combinations. For example, big data projects involving improving or speeding up decisions should probably be the responsibility of analytics people who are close to the business and the decision maker. The actual production implementation of such projects, however, must be the responsibility of the executive charged with making

FIGURE 3-2

Responsibility locus for big data projects

	Discovery	Production
Cost savings	IT innovation group	IT architecture and operations
Faster decisions	Business unit or function analytics group	Business unit or function executive
Better decisions	Business unit or function analytics group	Business unit or function executive
Product/service innovation	R&D or product development group	Product development or product management

or executing the decision. These responsibility loci are meant to be suggestive rather than definitive.

What Big Data Area to Address

Where should you look for opportunities to use big data successfully within your company? Most organizations should pursue a two-pronged approach in making this decision. One is to understand the opportunities available from a data perspective. Are you sitting on a goldmine of data that could shape or transform your strategy? If you're an insurance firm, perhaps you have a lot of claims data that hasn't been analyzed. If you work at a retail bank, there is undoubtedly a lot of data about consumer payments that you haven't done much with. If you work in manufacturing, there may well be data that is thrown off by manufacturing devices that you aren't using to optimize your process. Big data technologies may make it possible for you to analyze some of this unused data for the first time, and it could have a large impact on your business.

The other prong involves pursuing the big data applications that your business needs, rather than what is available. This is a time-honored strategic approach that involves going through your business strategy and noting goals, objectives, and initiatives that might be advanced through big data. Say, for example, that your strategy emphasizes doing a better job of predicting and meeting consumer demand. You may be able to identify some external data that could be mined for more accurate demand signals. Or if your strategic focus involves better management of your supply chain, you might be able to employ various possible forms of sensor data to get a better handle on where your inventory is and what conditions it is experiencing.

Neustar, a company that provides data management and analytics for large-volume telecommunications applications, provides a good example of pursuing both angles at once on this problem. The company historically (it spun out of Lockheed Martin) managed some important data and transactions, like North American phone numbers, number portability, several internet domains, GSM-format call and text routing, and so forth. Despite all the important data, these systems have never had a security breach.

But when Lisa Hook became CEO in 2010, she realized that the company could only go so far on telecom services.[11] She wanted to transition the company into one also focused on providing data, insights, and services outside of telecom. Some ideas for where to focus these services came from customers. Neustar began to ask for data services and customer insights based on the information it already had about its customers. Telecom firms wondered what their own data told them about whether particular customers were likely to skip out on paying their bills and should therefore be monitored more closely to avoid defaulting. Cable services firms wanted insights on the likelihood that a customer would be interested in upgrading to a triple-play package. Others wanted information about how to communicate with their customers more effectively. Hook saw a clear and growing demand for insights and analytics.

However, as Hook looked around her employee base, she saw a lot of people who could build and run huge, authoritative databases and very few people with a data science or analytics background. The answer to this skill shortage was right down the street from Neustar in northern Virginia. TARGUSinfo was a company with a similar focus on telecom that had already made the shift to a marketing analytics orientation. It understood the entire marketing process, from lead generation to retention, and could offer its customers assistance in this area. It had a very similar financial profile to Neustar, so Neustar acquired the company in October 2011.

The acquisition has worked out very well. TARGUSinfo already had a development process for data-driven products and services—a catalog of available data, governance, provenance, and permissible uses—and now Neustar is building one too. Neustar had lots of unstructured data—now housed in Hadoop clusters—and is exploring it to find out how best to turn it into products. To aid in this process, Neustar put a number of data scientists into a newly created Neustar Labs at the University of Illinois.

I asked Hook about Neustar's product development process— whether it started with its data and tried to find out what was of value in it, or started with its customer's needs and tried to find a solution in its data. It wasn't a quiz, but she gave what I consider the right answer: "Both. Sometimes simultaneously." And since she has people who understand the potential value in data and others who know customer needs, they can collaborate to develop new offerings.

How Rapidly to Move Out

The final dimension of your big data initiative I'll discuss is how rapidly and aggressively you should be moving. Should you jump in headfirst or put a cautious toe in the water? Should you have multiple projects or just one? Should you hire a group of data scientists or maybe rent one or two for a while? The answers to these questions depend on your industry, the activities of your competitors with big data, and how technically innovative your organization wants to be. I'll describe three overall levels of speed and aggressiveness in big data adoption (they are summarized in "What's the Right Speed of Big Data Adoption?").

What's the Right Speed of Big Data Adoption?

You should move conservatively if:

- Your competitors aren't doing much with big data.
- Technology hasn't driven industry transformation in the past.
- You don't have much data on customers or other important business entities.
- Your company typically isn't a first mover in industry innovation.

You should be moderately aggressive with big data if:

- Your industry is already active with big data or analytics.
- You want to stay ahead of competitors.
- Your company is typically facile with technology and data.
- You have at least some people who can do big data work.

You should be very aggressive if:

- Someone in your industry is already being very aggressive.
- You have been an analytical competitor in the past.
- You have used technology to transform your industry in the past.
- You have assembled all the necessary capabilities.

A Conservative Approach to Big Data

Almost every organization I can think of should at least be pursuing a conservative approach to big data. Conservatism may be warranted if you don't work directly with consumers, if your competitors aren't moving ahead on big data, if technology hasn't driven industry transformation in the past, or if your company generally lets others in the industry innovate first.

But even a conservative approach requires exploring the topic and its fit with your business or organizational model. The exploration should include both prongs of strategy described previously: an assessment of what types of large volume or unstructured data the organization might already have and what big data might be useful, given the current strategy. If you don't have the internal resources to do this sort of assessment, consultants from big data–oriented firms like Deloitte, Accenture, or IBM's Global Services division would be happy to help.

You may also need to undertake some management education about big data. I've been asked to speak not only to senior executives within companies but also to members of boards of directors, key partners, and large customers of companies. It's never too early to start shaping the views of key stakeholders, and some initiatives might even be codeveloped with partners.

The goal of these conservative efforts is to determine the likely course of big data in your business and industry and to start mobilizing interest and motivation to pursue it. But sooner rather than later, I suspect, the conditions for conservatism I've described will no longer prevail—a competitor will start advertising to hire data scientists, for example—and you'll want to take more aggressive actions.

A Moderately Aggressive Approach

A moderate approach is appropriate if your industry is already somewhat active with big data (I'd put travel and transportation, health care, consumer products, and consumer financial services in this category, for example) and you want to stay competitive without necessarily leading the charge. It's also appropriate if your industry is slow but you do want to be or stay in front.

A moderately aggressive approach means that you'd have a discovery capability that would be exploring several different projects, and at least one with a product/service innovation objective. You would expect one or two of these projects to move into production mode within a year or so. You should have already brought in some big data technology, such as a Hadoop cluster. Being moderately aggressive also means that you have established a data science capability and hired some people with that background.

A moderate approach also demands that you have worked out some of the organizational issues with big data. You have determined, for example, how your data scientists relate to more traditional quantitative analysts. You've given substantial thought to how a project moves from the discovery stage to the production stage. You have kept outright war from being declared by the traditional IT group against the big data group, or vice versa.

A Highly Ambitious Approach

Some of the companies I've described in this book, including GE, Amadeus, and online firms like Google, LinkedIn, and eBay, are taking a highly aggressive approach to big data. They have basically concluded, as Google chief economist Hal Varian once told me, "We're in the data business." For online businesses that generate vast amounts of clickstream data, that's an obvious conclusion; almost every industry leader is doing it. For makers of industrial products like GE, it's even more of an ambitious leap.

If you're planning to occupy this category of hardcore big data adopter, you need to have a lot of projects and a lot of capability, and it will cost you a lot of investment dollars. I've mentioned the multibillion-dollar investment at GE in a new center to do this sort of work. At Amadeus, almost every major function in the company is either exploring or in production with big data. LinkedIn, though it's still a relatively small company (with roughly seven thousand employees), has more than a hundred data scientists. Google has more than six hundred. These numbers bespeak a major commitment to big data.

You may want to accelerate your commitment levels into the "highly ambitious" category if your competitor is already in it. How would you feel, for example, if you were the CEO of Siemens (a traditional GE competitor in many of its industrial businesses), and you heard about GE's $2 billion investment in industrial big data? I haven't spoken with him, but I'm hoping he's giving the topic some serious thought. You may also be interested in exploring this level of commitment if big data is about to reshape your product category. For example, if I were Ford, GM, Fiat/Chrysler, Volkswagen, or any other large car company, I'd be petrified that Google was about to introduce its self-driving car. I would be putting a lot of energy and resources into matching, if not surpassing, Google's big data efforts in this category. Some automobile companies, notably Daimler, are already doing so.

In this chapter, I've tried to give you some tools for thinking about your organization's strategy for big data. You've now got at least four different objectives to choose among, two different stages of big data to consider, a couple of approaches to identifying applications, and three different levels of big data aggressiveness. In short, you're not lacking in options and in decisions your organization needs to make. But whatever your strategy and initiative portfolio with big data, you're going to need some smart people to help carry it out. That is the subject of the chapter 4.

Developing a Big Data Strategy

- Are you primarily interested in the cost advantages of big data, its ability to improve decision making, or its ability to help create new products and services?

- If your focus is decisions, is your goal primarily to make the same decisions faster or to make them better with more data and analysis?

- Do you have a portfolio that includes some projects meeting each of these objectives—some in discovery mode, others in production mode?

- Has your organization determined how aggressively it should be investing in big data and implementing new applications involving it?

- Is there anyone else in your industry—or related industries—who is investing more than you are in the technology?

4

The Human Side
of Big Data

If your goal is to make something good happen with big data in your organization, perhaps the most important component is the human one. After all, almost every other major factor of big data production is free or cheap. The software is often open source; the hardware is highly commoditized. The data is often either already lying around within your organization, or obtainable at little cost from, say, the internet. There are exceptions to this pattern, of course. But the humans who do big data work are difficult to find and keep, and expensive. And it's pretty clear that not much will happen without them.

Thus far the primary focus on the human side of big data has involved the data scientists, or the people who produce the applications and models. However, big data also means changes for those who manage and make decisions with it. And as always, senior managers set the tone for effective (or ineffective) efforts to harness big data. It's still early days for knowing a lot about the managerial issues with big data, but the topic is worthy of some discussion, and I'll address it later in the chapter.

In addition to describing the traits of data scientists and big data managers in this chapter, I'll also describe some approaches to hiring, retaining, and building these human capabilities. That's one of the most difficult issues for any organization committing to big data initiatives.

Are Data Scientists Really New?

Many times, when I interview managers of companies pursuing big data, they will argue that data scientists aren't really a new phenomenon. Certainly, many organizations have for decades employed quantitative analysts who also have to do a lot of work in data preparation and management. Blaise Heltai, a PhD in mathematics who taught math before going to work at Bell Labs in 1986 (and who is now a big data consultant), argued in an interview that he was doing the work of a data scientist at that august institution:

> We had to extract data from complex technologies before
> we could analyze it—often using the same kind of scripting
> languages as people use today. The volumes of data were often
> quite large—I remember analyzing phone access charges using
> call detail from a certain class of central office telecom switches,
> and it was a classic big data problem. We did a lot of modeling
> and optimization in finance and call routing. As with some big
> data projects today, we worked on new product offerings as well.
> We did demand experiments and economic modeling for new
> telecom services, managed field trials or new services, did the
> first smartphone tests, and performed the first successful video

on demand trial. All the elements of big data and data science were there, so I would argue that data scientists have been around for a while.[1]

My view is that while these skills definitely existed in the past—and could occasionally be found in one person—they were not as prevalent. Bell Labs and a few other science-oriented organizations may have had them, but many more organizations have and want them today. Let's refer to today's situation as a dramatic acceleration in demand for data scientists, rather than the pure invention of the role.

The Classic Data Scientist Model

The data scientist role started to become much more pervasive in the late 2000s in organizations, primarily in the San Francisco Bay area, that were engaged in harnessing online and social media data. It was a heady time; companies were piling up data and a variety of new technologies were coming along (many invented by data scientists) to store, process, and analyze it.

Key to the data scientist model was the idea that all the necessary skills were available in one person. Now there clearly are some of those people out there, and I will describe some of them. But since there aren't many, after chronicling the attributes and exploits of these heroic characters, I'll describe some more realistic approaches to assembling the necessary skills.

The classic data scientist has five key traits: hacker, scientist, quantitative analyst, trusted adviser, business expert (see "Traits of Data Scientists"). Let's look at each one of these traits individually before discussing their combination in real people.

Traits of Data Scientists

Hacker

- Ability to code

- Understanding of big data technology architectures

Scientist

- Evidence-based decision making

- Improvisation

- Impatience and action orientation

Trusted adviser

- Strong communication and relationship skills

- Ability to frame decisions and understand decision processes

Quantitative analyst

- Statistical analysis

- Visual analytics

- Machine learning

- Analysis of unstructured data, such as text, video, or images

Business expert

- Know how the business works and makes money

- Good sense of where to apply analytics and big data

Hacker

Because big data technologies are new, and because it's seldom easy to extract data from the places in which it resides and transform it for analysis, you have to be a bit of a hacker to succeed as a data scientist.

You have to be able to code or program above all; one chief data scientist told me that "Can you code?" was the first question he asked of prospective data scientist hires. Experience in any programming language is useful, but the best ones to know are scripting languages like Python, Hive, and Pig, or the language that they sometimes generate, Java. These scripting languages are relatively easy to program in, and have features for splitting large data processing problems across a distributed MapReduce framework.

The hacker component of data science also demands some familiarity with common big data technologies. The most important of these is the Hadoop/MapReduce family, including how they are implemented and scaled, and whether they should be offered on premises or in the cloud. These technologies are new and evolving quickly, so a data scientist should be open—indeed, aggressively open—to learning new tools and approaches.

Of course, hacking is only useful when undertaken in a valuable business context. As Jake Porway, a data scientist who focuses on nonprofit applications of big data, blogged about a conversation on the subject of *hackathons*, which are marathon programming sessions that many start-up and online companies organize in hope of finding creative insights from or uses for data:

> "We have a lot of data, but we have no idea what we should do with it." The director of the foundation looked plaintively across the table at me. "We were thinking of having a hackathon, or maybe running an app competition," he smiled. His co-workers nodded eagerly. I shuddered.
>
> I have this conversation about once a week. Awash in data, an organization—be it a healthcare nonprofit, a government agency, or a tech company—desperately wants to capitalize on the insights that the "Big Data" hype has promised them.

Increasingly, they are turning to hackathons—weekend events where coders, data geeks, and designers conspire to build software solutions in just 48 hours—to get new ideas and fill their capacity gap. There's a lot to be said for hackathons: They give the technology community great social opportunities and reward them with money and fame for their solutions, and companies get free access to a community of diligent experts they otherwise wouldn't know how to reach. For all of these upsides, however, hackathons are not ideal for solving big problems like reducing poverty, reforming politics, or improving education and, when they're used to interpret data for social impact, they can be downright dangerous . . .

Any data scientist worth their salary will tell you that you should start with a question, NOT the data. Unfortunately, data hackathons often lack clear problem definitions. Most companies think that if you can just get hackers, pizza, and data together in a room, magic will happen. This is the same as if Habitat for Humanity gathered its volunteers around a pile of wood and said, "Have at it!" By the end of the day you'd be left with a half of a sunroom with 14 outlets in it.[2]

In other words, hackathons may be a heck of an idea for producing new ideas, but they'll be much more valuable if they're targeted at real business problems.

The final word on the hacker skill is that there is a reason why many large companies don't hire hackers. *Hacking* is generally defined in this context as creative, rapid computing, but the term has an "outlaw" connotation—a tendency to get around the normal rules of computational behavior. Some hacking in the latter sense is probably necessary in the current Wild West days of big data. However, be careful that the hacker trait isn't the dominant one in a data scientist, or you may regret it. Hardcore hackers may cause more problems than the benefits they provide. They also may not have an interest in working for large, bureaucratic organizations.

Scientist

The *scientist* attribute of data scientists doesn't necessarily mean that they have to have been practicing scientists. Many have been, however; in my 2012 interviews with thirty data scientists, I discovered that 57 percent had PhDs in scientific or technical fields, and 90 percent had at least one degree in a scientific or technical field. The most common background was a PhD in experimental physics. Others held advanced degrees in biology, ecology, or social sciences that typically require a lot of computer work.

Does data science require detailed knowledge of these fields? Absolutely not. What a PhD in experimental physics has that's important to the data scientist role is not the degree or the specific knowledge involved in it, but an aptitude and attitude for tasks that are involved in data science. The aptitude involves the ability to construct experiments, to design experimental apparatus, and to gather, analyze, and describe the results from data. It's unlikely that the data analyzed by a scientist will have been really big—universities have seldom had access to really big data in the past—but it may well have been somewhat unstructured.

The attitudes likely to be present in scientists that come in handy with big data are a focus on evidence-based decisions, improvisation, impatience, and comfort with do-it-yourself. These are important skills in the early phases of big data work, when data scientists have to perform many groundbreaking activities that may later be performed much more easily by software. Scientists are also likely to be fast learners and able to absorb and master new technologies quickly.

However, it's actually rather wasteful for a smart person to spend four to six years getting a PhD in experimental physics (for example), and then to go into a data science role. Sure, such people are likely to possess many of the necessary skills. But they also know a lot that they don't need to know in data science, and there is little evidence that writing a PhD dissertation is a useful activity for aspiring data scientists. Eventually, we'll be able to procure the needed skills much more efficiently in master's-level programs specifically in data science, but right now scientists are the most likely source.

It should be pointed out, however, that many successful data scientists have no graduate degrees at all. Many of the skills are self-taught anyway; no university offered courses in them until recently. For example, Jeff Hammerbacher, a leading data scientist who with DJ Patil (then working at LinkedIn) coined the term *data scientist* while he worked at Facebook, has only an undergraduate degree. As I will argue in chapter 6, a big data culture is a meritocratic one—not one that insists on a certain type of degree to practice data science.

Trusted Adviser

Like traditional quantitative analysts, data scientists need strong communications and relationship skills. Also, like traditional quants, they are unlikely to have them! If you have gone to the effort to learn a lot about computers and statistics and data, you may have less interest in learning about human relationships.

But strong relationship skills are surely necessary. Data scientists are called on to advise senior executives about internal decisions. In companies where data is the product, they are called on to advise product and marketing leaders on data-based product and service opportunities. DJ Patil, one of the earliest people to be called a data scientist (in part because he codeveloped the term), likes to say that data scientists need to be "on the bridge" advising the captain at close range. If there are intermediaries between data scientists and decision makers, the decision makers may not understand all the important data and analytics issues involved in a key decision.

There is some evidence that these skills are important. A Gartner study found that "between 70 percent and 80 percent of corporate business intelligence projects fail" owing to "a combination of poor communications between IT and the business, the failure to ask the right questions or to think about the real needs of the business."[3] And granted, business intelligence projects usually involve small rather than big data. However, while the specific percentage of projects that fail is questionable, there is no doubt that lack of communication in small and big data projects causes big problems.

I won't go into great detail on this topic, because I've coauthored a book called *Keeping Up with the Quants* that deals with it extensively.[4] I don't think there are major differences between the communication and trusted adviser skills of small data quants and data scientists; these skills are highly necessary in both jobs.

Quantitative Analyst

After big data has been captured and "tamed" (converted from unstructured to structured data if necessary), it must be analyzed in the traditional fashion. So a data scientist also needs to be a quantitative analyst—to know his or her way around a variety of mathematical and statistical techniques and to be able to explain them easily and well to non-technical people. I and many other authors have written a lot about these statistical skills, so there is no point in rehashing them here.

There are, however, some differences between analytics as practiced on small, unstructured data, and those used on big data. One is that the idea of *statistical inference*—generalizing results from small samples to much larger populations—may be less essential. With big data, organizations are often analyzing the entire population of data, simply because the technology makes it possible. If you're not inferring results from a sample to a population, you no longer have to worry about such concepts as statistical significance, or the probability that the observed results represent the population (since they *are* the population). Still, however, I believe that we will continue to use samples in many cases. It's not feasible, for example, to ask all the citizens of the United States (or any other country, for that matter) what they think about political or social questions, so we'll still use survey samples for that purpose. And even if you have a ton of online data to analyze, it still may only represent a sample of customer usage defined by a particular time interval.

Another difference is a widespread preference for visual analytics on big data. For reasons not entirely understood (by anyone, I think), the results of big data analyses are often expressed in visual formats. Now, visual analytics have a lot of strengths: They are relatively easy for non-quantitative executives to interpret, and they get attention. The downside is that they are not generally well suited for expressing complex multivariate relationships and statistical models. Put in other terms, most visual displays of data are for descriptive analytics, rather than predictive or prescriptive ones. They can, however, show a lot of data at once, as figure 4-1 illustrates. It's a display of the tweets and retweets on Twitter involving particular *New York Times* articles.[5] I find—as with many other complex big data visualizations—this one difficult to decipher. I sometimes think that many big data visualizations are created simply because they can be, rather than to provide clarity on an issue.

FIGURE 4-1

Visual analytics on account closure factors in a bank

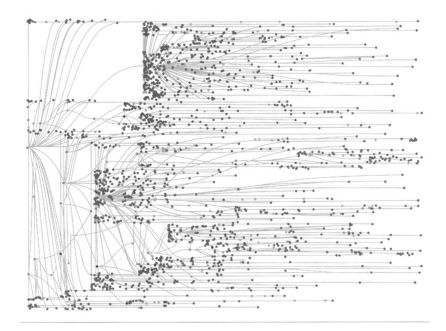

Why is it that visual analytics are common with big data? There are several possible explanations. One is the "big data = small math" hypothesis. It suggests that the effort to capture and structure data is so great with big data that there is little time or energy left to do complex multivariate statistics on it. There is only an ability to create simple frequency counts and then pictures and scatter plots based on them. This syndrome is well known within the data scientist community, but it is difficult to know just how important and pervasive it is.

Another explanation for the prominence of visual analytics in big data is that the two phenomena—big data and much more appealing visual analytics—arose at roughly the same time. Finally, there is the explanation that big data work is exploratory and iterative, so visual analytics are needed to explore the data and communicate preliminary findings to managers and decision makers. We may never know which of these explanations is more important, but the fact is that data scientists need to know something about visual display of data and analyses.

Machine learning is another analytical technique that data scientists should be somewhat knowledgeable about. As I describe in chapter 5, it involves automated testing and fitting of various models to a data set to find the best fit. It's really only semiautomated, however, because an analyst usually has to tell a machine learning program where to start and what varieties of data transformations to explore. Although it's often difficult, analysts should also try to interpret the results of machine learning analyses—to "look into the black box," if you will—and try to make sense of why a particular model fits the best. If the analyst can deduce a reason for why a particular model was the best fit, it will make it much easier to explain the results to decision makers and executives. But if you're talking about producing thousands of models a week, this sort of human interpretation is unlikely. In any case, many organizations that work with big data employ specialists in machine learning.

Big data often involves the processing of unstructured data types like text, images, and video. It is probably impossible for a data scientist to be familiar with the analysis of all of these data types, but a knowledge of analytical approaches to one of them would be very useful. For example, *natural language processing* (NLP) is a set of approaches to extracting meaning from text. It may involve counting, classifying, translating, or otherwise analyzing words. It's quite commonly used, for example, in understanding what customers are saying about a product or company. Virtually every large firm that is interested in big data should have someone available with NLP skills, but one or two experts will probably be sufficient.

Business Expert

Last but not least, it's important for data scientists to know a substantial amount about how the business works, or at least the part of it in which they will be engaged. How does the company make money? Who are its competitors? How does a company create successful products and services in the industry? And what are some of the key problems that can best be solved through big data and analytics? These are some of the questions to which an effective data scientist should have answers.

The knowledge will enable the data scientist to generate hypotheses and test them quickly and to provide solutions to key functional and business problems. Otherwise, it will be very difficult for him or her to add value to the business. It's the *application* of analytics to business problems that makes them useful (with big data or traditional analytics), so an interest in and experience with the relevant business context is important. Of course, data scientists may sometimes move across industries, and no one can be an expert in every type of business. However, it's very important that they have a strong curiosity about and interest in learning about the new business context into which they have entered. Data scientists are almost by definition very intelligent, so if they are also motivated to learn about a new business, they will pick it up quickly. But if you're interviewing one from another industry, make sure that the candidate shows interest and demonstrated business problem-solving ability in the industry from which he or she comes.

Horizontal versus Vertical Data Scientists

There are, of course, many types of data scientists. One way to characterize an important set of differences between types has been coined by Vincent Granville, who operates Data Science Central, a social network for data scientists like himself. In a blog post (with some analytical jargon you can toss around at cocktail parties), he described the difference between vertical and horizontal data scientists:

- Vertical data scientists have very deep knowledge in some narrow field. They might be computer scientists very familiar with computational complexity of all sorting algorithms. Or a statistician who knows everything about eigenvalues, singular value decomposition and its numerical stability, and asymptotic convergence of maximum pseudo-likelihood estimators. Or a software engineer with years of experience writing Python code (including graphic libraries) applied to API development and web crawling technology. Or a database guy with strong data modeling, data warehousing, graph databases, Hadoop and NoSQL expertise. Or a predictive modeler expert in Bayesian networks, SAS and SVM.

- Horizontal data scientists are a blend of business analysts, statisticians, computer scientists and domain experts. They combine vision with technical knowledge. They might not be expert in eigenvalues, generalized linear models and other semi-obsolete statistical techniques, but they know about more modern, data-driven techniques applicable to unstructured, streaming, and big data . . . They can design robust, efficient, simple, replicable and scalable code and algorithms.[6]

It's pretty clear from the tone that Granville has a preference for the horizontal variety. He argues that their broad, pragmatic knowledge is better than the deep knowledge of the vertical variety. I would have to agree; if you need the deep knowledge in a particular technique, you can probably hire a consultant in that domain. Mark Grabb at GE, a senior data scientist who is responsible for hiring other data scientists, also shares the preference for the horizontal types:

> Do we fully embrace the power that comes from the division of labor, looking for technologists with deep expertise resulting from years focused on a narrow area, and rely on strong communication across the team? We have found such experts to be valuable, but more often we have found their value to be realized in building new analytical tools for the Data Scientists and not playing the role of the Data Scientist. These singularly focused experts, too often, lack the business speed and desire to create a new solution from existing tools, and such experts often take pride and want to be valued for developing new capability.[7]

The Team Approach

The problem with assembling all the skills I've just described in one Superman or Supergirl (there is no official "Superwoman" in the comics) is that there aren't very many of them. Put in probabilistic terms, if you're looking for the top 1 percent in each of these skills—and if we assume that the skills are distributed independently of each other—your chance of finding one with all five skills is .00000000001. And remember that even if you find that human in the haystack, he or she may not be interested in working for you.

The other complicating factor in focusing on multitalented individuals is that data scientists—the horizontal variety in particular—are only one component of an effective approach to big data projects. There is, for example, a heavy data hygiene component—extracting, cleaning, and reconciling data before it can be analyzed. Data people in IT functions have done this work for decades, and the need has never gone away. A 2012 study by Talent Analytics surveyed 302 quantitative analysts and data scientists. Among other topics, it addressed the specific job activities of analytical professionals. It found that "data preparation" was a key and common task for people who call themselves analysts and data scientists. Actual data analysis and visual display of results took up a relatively small amount of the time spent by analytical professionals.[8]

The obvious alternative to the multirole data scientist is to assemble a team with all the necessary skills—to find one person who is really great at hacking data, another with strong statistical skills, and so forth. Some organizations try to find people with 1.5 or 2.5 of the necessary skills, and through training or experience try to build some of the rest. Those with one skill, for example, need to respect people with other skills and acknowledge the need for those skills. It will take a good data science manager to cultivate and nurture this sort of respect. Mark Grabb, technology leader, analytics, at GE Global Research, describes GE's experience with hiring people with multiple skills:

> At GE, we are finding that Data Scientists that have expertise in two or three areas are the most effective, and we are finding this to be true for a few reasons. First, there seems to be a tremendous creative advantage in knowing multiple areas. I have heard this referred to as the "coign of vantage." A coign, a word that may have fallen out of the dictionary in recent decades, in this sense, should be thought as the cornerstone of a building. One that stands at the exterior corner of a building has the advantage of seeing two sides, albeit not all sides, of the building, leading to a tremendous creative advantage over the person that can only see one side. It's the same thing with Data Scientists. Second, we have observed that most analytical experts that highly specialize in one area are more likely to be less effective as collaborators, and

effective Data Scientists must be collaborative. A compounding disadvantage is that more narrow experts require more required channels of communication, and they may have a personality type that doesn't embrace collaboration. Third, we have concluded that expertise comes with dedication, study, and application (a testament to the 10,000 hour rule, learned from reading Malcolm Gladwell's books), so expecting to hire and train hundreds of people that know it all simply isn't practical.[9]

Given the diversity of skills needed, the manager of data scientists will also have to be good at assembling teams with the needed skills for each project. Some projects will require more data capabilities, others more analytical skills, and so forth. The data science manager will have to determine the specific needs of the project before assembling the team.

Opera Solutions, a big data consulting firm, employs the team approach to data science on its projects with its clients. The company's projects include hands-on data scientists whose jobs it is to create new algorithms; analytics managers who provide guidance to the scientists about the business problem at hand; and traditional project managers, who manage the cost, scheduling, and deliverables of the project. In addition, there are often experts in a particular industry—either a business head or a science head—who advise the project about the particular data and analytical needs of that industry.

Where Do You Get Data Scientists?

Data Scientists from Universities

I noted earlier that data scientists today often have advanced degrees in science, but that won't always be the most efficient way to procure the necessary skills. How soon will there be more direct educational paths to data science? Well, as I write I believe there is no university that has yet issued a degree in data science. But there are: (a) a growing number of courses in the field and (b) a growing number of institutions that are planning data science degree programs. The degree programs are primarily master's-level programs; the School of Information at the University of California, Berkeley, and New York University, for example, have announced them. Universities are not fast-moving institutions, but they have been getting the message that businesses and other organizations need these people. Within a couple of years, there should be plenty of programs; and a year or two after that, plenty of data science graduates.

What if you need people sooner than that? You can still benefit from university-educated candidates, but they may not have the degree-based certification that makes it easier to know whom to hire. As I mentioned, several schools offer courses and even degrees on big data, machine learning, programming in scripting languages like Python, and other relevant skills. Some, like Stanford and MIT, offer them online.

Another option is to tap the large and fast-growing number of programs in business analytics. They include North Carolina State (the granddaddy of them all), Northwestern, New York University, Stevens, Louisiana State University, and the Universities of Tennessee, Alabama, Cincinnati, and San Francisco. One list, compiled by Barbara Wixom at the University of Virginia and several other academics, identified fifty-nine universities with degrees or majors in business intelligence or business analytics.[10] Many of these programs have added, or are planning to add, data science content to their programs.

If you're a university professor or administrator surveying this landscape, you should attend to some of the findings from an employer survey (446 employers) by Wixom and her coauthors. They found that the most desired skill was communications, followed by the expected technical and analytics skills. "Communications" doesn't mean expertise in (for example) the TCP/IP communications protocol, but rather the ability to communicate the results of analyses effectively to decision makers. The biggest obstacle to hiring reported by the employers was a lack of business experience—so schools should crank up those internship programs.

If you're a company needing data scientists—now or in the future—don't sit by passively and wait for students to be churned out. Work with universities now to tell them what skills you want. Offer internships in your company; not only is it (usually) free labor, but you can identify the best students for later hiring. Offer professors some data sets (ideally, really big ones) for students to work on. And if you really want influence at a local university, it never hurts to toss a few dollars their way to finance a research project or an internship program.

Non-University Sources

There are a variety of other approaches in use to develop and hire data scientists. EMC, for example, has determined that the availability of data scientists will be an important gating factor in its own big data efforts and those of its customers. So it has created a Data Science and Data Analytics training program for its employees and customers. The organization has already begun to put graduates of the program to work on internal big data projects, and has also made the course materials available to universities. IBM has a similar program. Deloitte has worked with the Kelley School of Business at the University of Indiana to develop big data and analytics skills in its employees.

Given the difficulty of finding and keeping data scientists, one would think that a good strategy would involve hiring them as consultants. Yet many firms that are aggressively pursuing big data projects seem to want to employ their own data scientists (perhaps because they are worried about turning over their important data assets to outside firms). In recent months, however, I have seen both an increase in demand for data scientists from consulting organizations, particularly from large organization clients. And as I hinted in chapter 3, firms such as Accenture, Deloitte, and IBM have begun to hire and train data scientists in larger numbers. Predominantly offshore firms such as Mu Sigma, a "math factory" with thousands of quants as employees, are also hiring data scientists in considerable numbers.

One data scientist has come up with a creative approach to training new data scientists. The Insight Data Science Fellows Program, started by Jake Klamka (whose academic background is high-energy physics), takes scientists for six weeks and teaches them the skills to be a data scientist. The program includes mentoring by local companies with big data challenges (e.g., Facebook, Twitter, Google, LinkedIn). "I originally was aiming for ten fellows. I had over two hundred applicants and accepted thirty of them," says Klamka. "The demand from companies has been phenomenal; they just can't get this kind of high-quality talent."[11]

Venture capital firms are also entering the data science game. In order to help the demand by companies in its portfolio, Greylock Partners, an early-stage venture firm that has backed companies like Facebook, LinkedIn, Palo Alto Networks, and Workday, has built a recruiting team that focuses in part on data scientists. Dan Portillo, who leads the team, says, "The demand [for] data scientists is at an all-time high from our later-stage companies. Once they have data, they really need people who can manage it and find insights in it. The traditional backgrounds of people you saw ten to fifteen years ago just don't cut it these days."[12]

Retention of Data Scientists

Once they are hired or created, companies may also face issues in retaining data scientists. Several of those I interviewed in online firms or small start-ups had changed jobs several times in the past year. One commented, "After about a year, it often becomes clear that there is nothing left for me to do." (Presumably, that data scientist is brought in for a single project, and it is done after a year.) Another noted, "Data scientists receive lots of job offers—sometimes I get two or three calls a week from headhunters. It's not surprising that with so much opportunity there is a lot of movement."

While I know of no studies on how to retain data scientists, the usual approaches—money, relationships, good bosses—are probably effective. If you are from a large company and have hired data scientists, make sure that they are not only working directly with business functions and units, but also with other data science and analytics people. Given the strong need for intellectual stimulation and growth, however, the most important way to retain a data scientist is to provide him or her with good data and interesting problems to solve.

In my interviews with data scientists, the issue of impact cropped up frequently. They want to use data to have a substantial impact on the world. They view this as a unique period in history in which there are huge data sets and very powerful tools. As Amy Heineike, a prominent data scientist at the start-up Quid in San Francisco, put it in an interview:

> If you have access to the data and the tools, you can already find out some really cool stuff, but we are just scratching the surface. What inspires me is the opportunity to create something really interesting. Could something be important, have impact, or reach a lot of people? I am also interested in how to include data scientists within a diverse engineering team and company, and in combining the diverse skills that make up an effective data science team. So when I evaluate an opportunity, I look for a rich data set that the company has to work with, or an important question for which we might be able to find data. And I want to make sure that there are the resources and senior management support available to support the data science function.[13]

Another data scientist I interviewed noted that he and his colleagues are motivated by—and highly attuned to—the attitudes of the founders of their company: "The key issue is, how analytical are the founders? How ambitious and open-minded are they? That's ultimately the deciding factor in how analytical the organization becomes. If they're just oriented to the technology and the engineering, it won't happen."

Although they are usually well paid, data scientists seem more motivated by the challenge and impact of the work than by money. One commented, "If we wanted to work with structured data, we'd be on Wall Street." Indeed, it seems likely that the quants who went to Wall Street in substantial numbers in the 1990s are the same types of people who become data scientists today.

Data scientists—at least those I interviewed in online and start-up firms—also see creating a product as far more motivating than simply advising a decision maker. One described being a consultant as "the dead zone—all you get to do is tell someone else what the analyses say they should do." They view working on products or processes for customers as having much more potential impact. They see creating a product feature, or at least a demo of it, as far more valuable than creating a PowerPoint presentation or a report for management.

Big Data Skills for Managers

Data scientists aren't the only human concern in the management and analysis of big data; there is also an important impact on decision making by managers and executives. (Managers also play a leadership and culture-building role with regard to big data, but I will discuss that in chapter 6.)

As I've discussed in previous chapters, big data is sometimes used for purposes of product development or cost reduction rather than internal decision making within organizations. However, when it does support decisions, the volume and velocity of big data is such that conventional, high-certitude approaches to decision making are often not appropriate. By the time an organization has achieved a high level of certitude about the insights and the implications, much more new data would have become available. Therefore, many organizations must adopt a more continuous, more indicative, less certain approach to analysis and decision making.

Social media analytics, for example, are rarely definitive; instead, they provide fast-breaking trends on customer sentiments about products, brands, and companies. It might be useful to determine with certainty whether an hour's or a day's online content is correlated with sales changes, but by the time that analysis would be completed, much more new content would have arrived. It's important then, to have clear criteria for what decisions to make and what actions to take based on big data analyses—particularly in fast-changing domains like social analytics.

Sometimes it's important to admit that the data and analyses are not definitive. I've already talked about the IIunchWorks project at the United Nations, which seeks to identify trends and hunches at an early stage in order to decide whether they merit further attention. This could also be the right approach for social sentiment analysis—to use it as a tip-off that further investigation is required, rather than a specific action.

If you're a little more certain—but not entirely—that something important is going on based on your big data analysis, you might consider an automated recommendation. If necessary, a human could override it. That's the approach that some health-care organizations are planning to take with the recommendations of IBM's Watson system, for example. Here's one account of the Watson implementation in health insurer WellPoint: "Interestingly, if Watson concludes that a physician or provider's treatment request is not the most effective one based on a patient's history and medical benefits, the computer can register its disagreement—but . . . it cannot override the provider's decision or deny treatment requests. Instead, a human nurse would have to review Watson's alternative suggestion, and then make a judgment call along with the provider on whether or not to comply with it."[14]

Not just individual managers' decisions need to change in the big data world. More broadly, organizations managing big data need to view data management, analysis, and decision making in terms of "industrialized" flows and processes, rather than discrete stocks of data or events. Historically, data analysis required significant time and human intervention. Once data was identified, it was extracted and loaded into a data warehouse, and then analysts went to work. Typically, the analysts would take significant time in massaging, analyzing, and interpreting the data. In many cases, they would report it out in visual formats for better understanding by decision makers.

However, the volume and velocity of big data means that organizations must develop continuous processes for gathering, analyzing, interpreting, and acting on data—at least for operational applications such as multichannel customer "next best offers," identifying fraud in real time, and scoring medical patients for health risk. Much analysis, and at least some decision making, must be automated or semiautomated. This will mean integration into so-called decision management or business process management tools, and some vendors, such as IBM and Pegasystems, are moving their software offerings in the direction of this integration. Decision management expert James Taylor has explored this issue as well in books and blog posts.[15]

For example, PNC Bank has been working with Pegasystems software to create well-structured and semiautomated processes for customer service and offers across all customer contact points and channels.[16] PNC began implementing this software three years ago to create a consistent approach to customer offers and relationships—initially through inbound channels, but eventually through outbound ones as well. The bank already makes available a million offer decisions a day in customer interactions through all major channels. Most of the time, a call center agent is advised to simply expedite the call based on predicted value of the additional talk time. Branch personnel typically have a little more time and context to present the recommended offer for other banking services and products. Each insight and recommendation is targeted according to the customer's purchasing power and previous behaviors. The analytical models are typically developed offline in SAS or through real-time modeling capability and applied through the Pegasystems engine. In part because of this capability, PNC was recently rated first among sixteen financial institutions for online marketing and promotion by Corporate Insight, a banking research and consulting firm.

As I mentioned previously in this chapter, big data analyses often involve reporting of data in visual formats. While there are increasing technological capabilities for displaying data in dashboards and visual analytics, visual analytics often require considerable human interpretation—and that takes up valuable time. The time and expense of such human interpretation may be difficult to justify in operationally intense big data environments. As much as possible, humans should be eliminated from operational big data processes, or their involvement limited to initial development of rules and scoring algorithms and dealing with overrides to recommendations and exceptions. Of course, there will still be a role for detailed human analysis in research and exploration-oriented applications, but these contexts will typically involve slower analysis and decision processes.

In big data environments involving increased speed of decision making (sometimes called *high-performance analytics*), the technology allows for much faster analysis of data. But if organizations are to receive value, they need to determine what to do with the additional time that has been freed up. Can they, for example, do more analyses to refine their models? One retail company was spending five hours to develop a single algorithm model each day for new customer acquisition. Using big data technologies, the company reduced the model processing time to only three minutes, allowing a model to be iterated every thirty minutes or so while also using multiple modeling techniques. This improved the model lift from 1.6 percent to 2.5 percent—a seemingly small improvement, but one that could pay off dramatically across many customers. Other ways to refine models with big data include using more data, incorporating more variables, and trying to fit more varieties of models through machine learning approaches.

Some other companies are attempting to improve the entire process in which the big data analysis takes place. The key to this is accelerating decisions and actions to match the increased speed of analysis.

Humans and Big Data

I hope it's obvious by now that the skills of talented human beings are the single most important resource in successfully exploiting big data. They extract the data from obscure locations, write programs to turn unstructured into structured data, analyze the data, interpret the results, and advise executives on what to do about it—all in short order and with a sense of urgency.

Occasionally, I hear predictions that data scientists will be less necessary in the future because computers and software will take over many data science functions. "Machine learning will eliminate the need for human analysts," some argue. A few software vendors claim to be creating "data scientists in a box." I am sure that technology will advance in the area of big data management and analysis, but I don't think the smart humans will go away. I've found that even companies that are aggressively pursuing automation-oriented technologies (e.g., machine learning) discover that they need to hire a lot of machine learning specialists.

I have been hearing for decades that we will need fewer quantitative analysts in the future, but it never seems to happen. In fact, among the hundreds of organizations I have engaged with in education, consulting, or research, there is a perfect correlation between two variables: how many really smart people they have doing analytics work and the level of their analytical capabilities. I don't see that correlation changing in the big data world. I suspect that the trend of hiring more and more analytics and data sciences people—as depicted in figure 4-2—will continue at its amazing pace.

FIGURE 4-2

Analytics and data science job growth, 1991–2011

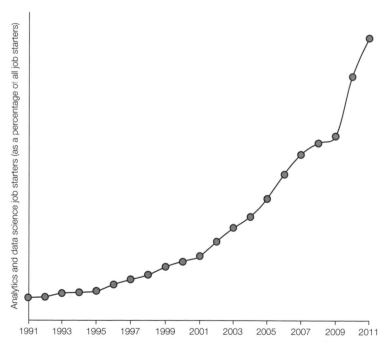

Source: LinkedIn Analytics.

The Human Side of Big Data

- Do you have individual workers or teams who are hybrids of hacker, scientist, quantitative analyst, trusted adviser, and business expert?

- What is your primary sourcing strategy for such people? Do you intend to recruit them externally or develop them internally, for example? If you plan to rely on consultants, do you have some in mind that possess the needed skills?

- How do you plan to retain the people or teams with data science skills that you do have?

- Do you have relationships with universities that offer big data–related instruction?

- Are you beginning to think about how to retrain managers to analyze, decide, and act effectively in a world of big data?

Technology for Big Data

Written with Jill Dyché

A major component of what makes the management and analysis of big data possible is new technology.* In effect, big data is not just a large volume of unstructured data, but also the technologies that make processing and analyzing it possible. Specific big data technologies analyze textual, video, and audio content. When big data is fast moving, technologies like machine learning allow for the rapid creation of statistical models that fit, optimize, and predict the data. This chapter is devoted to all of these big data technologies and the difference they make. The technologies addressed in the chapter are outlined in table 5-1.

---

*I am indebted in this section to Jill Dyché, vice president of SAS Best Practices, who collaborated with me on this work and developed many of the frameworks in this section. Much of the content is taken from our report, *Big Data in Big Companies* (International Institute for Analytics, April 2013).

TABLE 5-1

Overview of technologies for big data

Technology	Definition
Hadoop	Open-source software for processing big data across multiple parallel servers
MapReduce	The architectural framework on which Hadoop is based
Scripting languages	Programming languages that work well with big data (e.g., Python, Pig, Hive)
Machine learning	Software for rapidly finding the model that best fits a data set
Visual analytics	Display of analytical results in visual or graphic formats
Natural language processing (NLP)	Software for analyzing text—frequencies, meanings, etc.
In-memory analytics	Processing big data in computer memory for greater speed

If you are looking for hardcore detail about how big data technology works, you've come to the wrong place. My focus here is not on how Hadoop functions in detail, or whether Pig or Hive is the better scripting language (alas, such expertise is beyond my technological pay grade anyway). Instead, my focus will be on the overall technology architecture for big data and how it coexists with that for traditional data warehouses and analytics.

No single business trend in the last decade has as much potential impact on incumbent IT investments as big data. Indeed, big data promises—or threatens, depending on how you view it—to upend legacy technologies within many companies. The way that data is stored and processed for analysis, and the hardware and software for doing so, are being transformed by the technology solutions that are tied to big data. Some of that technology is truly new with big data, and some has been around for a while but is being applied in different ways. In the next section I'll distinguish between these technologies.

What's Really New about Big Data Technology?

Many discussions about what's really new about big data focus on the technology required to handle data in large volumes and unstructured formats. That is indeed new, but the fact that it's attracted most of the attention doesn't mean that it's the subject most deserving of your attention. What is ultimately important about big data technology is how it can bring value to your organization—lower the costs and increase the speed of processing data, develop new products or services, or allow new data and models for better decision making.

However, a few paragraphs here on big data structuring tools are worthwhile, simply because you as a manager will have to make decisions about whether or not to implement them within your organization. What's new about big data technologies is primarily that the data can't be handled well with traditional database software or with single servers. Traditional relational databases assume data in the form of neat rows and columns of numbers, and big data comes in a variety of diverse formats. Therefore, a new generation of data processing software has emerged to handle it. You'll hear people talking often about Hadoop, an open-source software tool set and framework for dividing up data across multiple computers; it is a unified storage and processing environment that is highly scalable to large and complex data volumes. Hadoop is sometimes called Apache Hadoop, because the most common version of it is supported by The Apache Software Foundation. However, as tends to happen with open-source projects, many commercial vendors have created their own versions of Hadoop as well. There are Cloudera Hadoop, Hortonworks Hadoop, EMC Hadoop, Intel Hadoop, Microsoft Hadoop, and many more.

One of the reasons Hadoop is necessary is that the volume of the big data means that it can't be processed quickly on a single server, no matter how powerful. Splitting a computing task—say, an algorithm that compares many different photos to a specified photo to try to find a match—across multiple servers can reduce processing time by a hundredfold or more. Fortunately, the rise of big data coincides with the rise of inexpensive commodity servers with many—sometimes thousands of—computer processors. Another commonly used tool is MapReduce, a Google-developed framework for dividing big data processing across a group of linked computer nodes. Hadoop contains a version of MapReduce.

These new technologies are by no means the only ones that organizations need to investigate. In fact, the technology environment for big data has changed dramatically over the past several years, and it will continue to do so. There are new forms of databases such as columnar (or vertical) databases; new programming languages—interactive scripting languages like Python, Pig, and Hive are particularly popular for big data; and new hardware architectures for processing data, such as big data appliances (specialized servers) and in-memory analytics (computing analytics entirely within a computer's memory, as opposed to moving on and off disk storage).

There is another key aspect of the big data technology environment that differs from traditional information management. In that previous world, the goal of data analysis was to segregate data into a separate pool for analysis—typically a data warehouse (which contains a wide variety of data sets addressing a variety of purposes and topics) or mart (which typically contains a smaller amount of data for a single purpose or business function). However, the volume and velocity of big data—remember, it can sometimes be described as a fast-moving river of information that never stops—means that it can rapidly overcome any segregation approach. Just to give one example: eBay, which collects a massive amount of online clickstream data from its customers, has more than 40 petabytes of data in its data warehouse—much more than most organizations would be willing to store. And it has much more data in a set of Hadoop clusters—nobody seems to know exactly (and the number changes daily), but well over 100 petabytes.

Therefore, in the big data technology environment, many organizations are using Hadoop and similar technologies to briefly store large quantities of data, and then flushing it out for new batches. The persistence of the data gives just enough time to do some (often rudimentary) analysis or exploration on it. This data management approach may not dethrone the enterprise data warehouse (EDW) approach, but it at least seems likely to supplement it.

There is good news and bad news in how to handle big data. The good news is that many big data technologies are free (as with open-source software) or relatively inexpensive (as with commodity servers). You may even be able to avoid capital expense altogether; the hardware and software technology are also often available in the cloud and can be bought "by the drink" at relatively low cost. The downside is that big data technologies are relatively labor-intensive to architect and program. They'll require a lot of attention from your technologists, and even some attention from you. It used to be that for most organizations, there was only one way to store data—a relational database on a mainframe. Today and for the foreseeable future, there are many new technologies to choose from, and you can't just write a big check to IBM, Oracle, Teradata, or SAP to cover them. In order to avoid making bad decisions, you and your organization must do some studying.

It's also important to point out what is not so new with big data, which is how it's analyzed. The technologies I've described thus far are used either to store big data or to transform it from an unstructured or semistructured format into the typical rows and columns of numbers. When it's in that format, it can be analyzed like any other data set, albeit larger. It may still be useful to employ multiple commodity servers to do the analysis, but the basic statistical and mathematical algorithms for doing the analysis haven't changed much at all.

These approaches for converting unstructured data into structured numbers are not entirely new either. For as long as we've been analyzing text, voice, and video data, for example, we've had to convert it into numbers for analysis. The numbers might convey how often a particular pattern of words or pixels appears in the data, or whether the text or voice sounds convey positive or negative sentiment. The only thing that's new about it is the speed and cost with which this conversion can be accomplished. It's important to remember, however, that such a conversion isn't useful until the data are summarized, analyzed, and correlated through analytics.

The tools that organizations use for big data analysis aren't that different from what has been used for data analysis in the past. They include basic statistical processing with either proprietary (e.g., SAS or SPSS) or open-source (e.g., R) statistical programs. However, instead of the traditional hypothesis-based approach to statistical analysis, in which the analyst or decision maker comes up with a hypothesis and then tests it for fit with the data, big data analysis is more likely to involve machine learning.

This approach, which might be referred to as *automated modeling*, fits a variety of different models to data in order to achieve the best possible fit. The benefit of machine learning is that it can very quickly generate models to explain and predict relationships in fast-moving data. The downside of machine learning is that it typically leads to results that are somewhat difficult to interpret and explain. All we know is that the computer program found that certain variables are important in the model, and it may be difficult to understand why. Nevertheless, the pace and volume of data in the big data world makes it important to employ machine learning in some situations.

The Big Data Stack

As with all strategic technology trends, big data introduces highly specialized features that set it apart from legacy systems. Figure 5-1 illustrates the typical components of the big data stack (layers of technology).

Each component of the stack is optimized around the large, unstructured or semistructured nature of big data. Working together, these moving parts comprise a holistic solution that's fine-tuned for specialized, high-performance processing and storage.

FIGURE 5-1

The big data stack

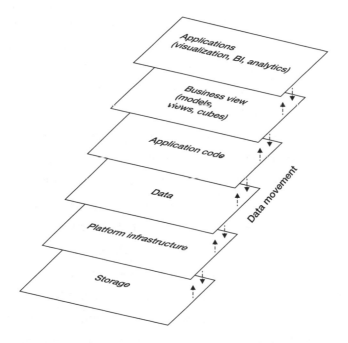

Source: SAS Best Practices, 2013.

Storage

There is nothing particularly distinctive about the storage of big data except its low cost. Storing large and diverse amounts of data on disk is becoming more cost-effective as the disk technologies become more commoditized and efficient. Storage in Hadoop environments is typically on multiple disks (solid state storage is still too expensive) attached to commodity servers. Companies like EMC sell storage solutions that allow disks to be added quickly and cheaply, thereby scaling storage in lock-step with growing data volumes. Indeed, many IT managers increasingly see Hadoop as a low-cost alternative for the archival and quick retrieval of large amounts of historical data.

Platform Infrastructure

The big data *platform* is typically the collection of functions that comprise high-performance processing of big data. The platform includes capabilities to integrate, manage, and apply sophisticated computational processing to the data. Typically, big data platforms include a Hadoop (or similar open-source project) foundation—you can think of it as big data's execution engine. It's often surprisingly capable, as Tim Riley, an information architect at insurance giant USAA, noted in an interview: "We knew there were a lot of opportunities for Hadoop when we started. So we loaded some data into Hadoop. After making some quick calculations, we realized that the data we'd just loaded would have exceeded the capacity of our data warehouse. It was impressive."[1]

Open-source technologies like Hadoop have become the de facto processing platform for big data. Indeed, the rise of big data technologies has meant that the conversation around analytics solutions has fundamentally changed. Companies unencumbered with legacy data warehouses (many recent high-tech start-ups among them) can now leverage a single Hadoop platform to segregate complex workloads and turn large volumes of unstructured data into structured data ready for analysis.

However, it would be inaccurate to view Hadoop as the last word in big data platform infrastructure. It was one of the first tools to serve this purpose, but there are already multiple alternatives, some new and some already well understood, and there will be many more new options in the future. In large firms, as I will describe later in this chapter, Hadoop may coexist with traditional enterprise data warehouse and data-mart-based platform infrastructures.

Data

The expanse of big data is as broad and complex as the applications for it. Big data can mean human genome sequences, oil-well sensors, cancer cell behaviors, locations of products on pallets, social media interactions, or patient vital signs, to name a few examples. The data layer in the stack implies that data is a separate asset, warranting discrete management and governance.

To that end, a 2013 survey of data management professionals found that of the 339 companies responding, 71 percent admitted that they "have yet to begin planning" their big data strategies.[2] The respondents cited concerns about data quality, reconciliation, timeliness, and security as significant barriers to big data adoption. Because it's new and somewhat experimental for many companies, the priority of big data management typically falls behind that for small data. If a company or industry is still wrestling with data integration and quality for fundamental transaction data, it may take a while to get to big data.

This is true in the health-care industry, for example, which is just putting in electronic medical record systems. Allen Naidoo, Vice President for Advanced Analytics at Carolinas HealthCare, observes, "It is challenging, but critically important, to prioritize the type of analytics we do while simultaneously integrating data, technologies, and other resources."[3] Indeed, the health-care provider has plans to add genetics data to its big data roadmap as soon as it formalizes some of the more complex governance and policy issues around the data.

But like Carolinas HealthCare, most companies are in the early stages of data governance approaches for big data. This was a hard enough problem for internal structured data; most organizations struggled with issues like, "Who owns our customer data," or "Who's got responsibility for updating our product master files." Since big data is often external to the organization (e.g., from the internet or the human genome or mobile phone location sensors), governance of it is often a tricky issue. Data ownership is much less clear, and responsibilities for ongoing data management haven't been defined either in most cases. We're going to be wrestling with big data governance for quite a while.

Application Code

Just as big data varies with the business application, the code used to manipulate and process the data can vary. Hadoop uses a processing framework called MapReduce not only to distribute data across the disks but also to apply complex computational instructions to that data. In keeping with the high-performance capabilities of the platform, MapReduce instructions are processed in parallel across various nodes on the big data platform, and then quickly assembled to provide a new data structure or answer set.

An example of a big data application in Hadoop might be "Find the number of all the influential customers who like us on social media." A text-mining application might crunch through social media transactions, searching for words such as *fan, love, bought,* or *awesome* and consolidating a list of key influencer customers with positive sentiment.

Apache Pig and Hive are two open-source scripting languages that sit on top of Hadoop and provide a higher-level language for carrying out MapReduce functionality in application code. Pig provides a scripting language for describing operations like reading, filtering, transforming, joining, and writing data; it is a higher-level language than Java (that is, Pig Latin, the Pig language, is translated into Java) and allows for higher programming productivity. Some other organizations use the Python open-source scripting language for this purpose. Hive performs similar functions but is more batch oriented, and it can transform data into the relational format suitable for Structured Query Language (SQL; used to access and manipulate data in databases) queries. This makes it useful for analysts who are familiar with that query language.

Business View

The *business view* layer of the stack makes big data ready for further analysis. Depending on the big data application, additional processing via MapReduce or custom code might be used to construct an intermediate data structure, such as a statistical model, a flat file, a relational table, or a data cube. The resulting structure may be intended for additional analysis or to be queried by a traditional SQL-based query tool. Many vendors are moving to so-called "SQL on Hadoop" approaches, simply because SQL has been used in business for a couple of decades, and many people (and higher-level languages) know how to create SQL queries. This business view ensures that big data is more consumable by the tools and the knowledge workers that already exist in an organization.

Applications

In this layer, the results of big data processing are analyzed and displayed either by business users or by other systems using them to make automated decisions. As I noted earlier in this chapter, the analysis of big data is not so different from traditional data analysis, except that it is more likely to be done with machine learning (automated model fitting tools), faster processing tools like in-memory and high-performance analytics environments, and visual analytics. All of those tools will come in handy at this level of the big data stack.

As I have mentioned, many consumers of big data (and for that matter, many consumers of traditional small data analytics) prefer it to be displayed visually. Unlike the specialized business intelligence technologies and unwieldy spreadsheets of yesterday, data visualization tools allow the average businessperson to view information in an intuitive, graphical way.

The data visualization shown in figure 5-2 displays two different views of the data. The first shows dropped calls by region and grouped by the generation of the network technology. The second shows that the distribution of dropped calls is different at each hour, such as a higher percentage of dropped calls in the 4G network around the call start hour of 17:00. This kind of information might prompt a network operator to drill down and discover the root causes of networks problems and which high-value customers might be affected by them.

Such a visualization can be pulled by the network operator onto her desktop PC or pushed to the mobile device of a service technician in the field, thereby decreasing time-to-resolution for high-impact trouble tickets. And it can be done in a fraction of the time it used to take finding, accessing, loading, and consolidating the data from myriad billing and customer systems.

Data visualizations, although normally highly appealing to managerial users, are more difficult to create when the primary output is a

FIGURE 5-2

Data visualization at a wireless carrier

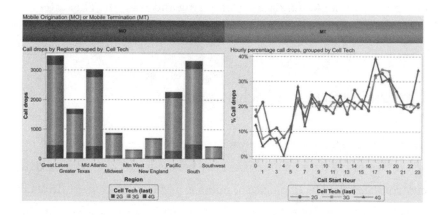

Source: SAS Visual Analytics.

multivariate predictive model; humans have difficulty understanding visualizations in more than two dimensions. Some data visualization programs now select the most appropriate visual display for the type of data and number of variables. Of course, if the primary output of a big data analysis is an automated decision, there is no need for visualization. Computers would prefer to get their inputs in numbers, not pictures!

Another possibility for the applications layer is to create an *automated narrative* in textual format. Users of big data often talk about "telling a story with data," but they don't often enough employ narrative (rather than graphic images) to do so. This approach, used by such companies as Narrative Sciences and Automated Insights, creates a story from raw data. Automated narrative was initially used by these companies to write journalistic accounts of sporting contests, but it is also being used for financial data, marketing data, and many other types. Its proponents don't argue that it will win the Nobel Prize in Literature, but they do think such tools are quite good at telling stories built around data—in some cases, better than humans.

This stack, of course, does not always appear in isolation. In large, established organizations, it must coexist and integrate with a variety of other technologies for data warehousing and analysis. That integration is the subject of the next section.

Integrating Big Data Technologies

Many large, established organizations today are interested in taking advantage of big data technologies, but have a variety of existing data environments and technologies to manage as well. For example, in their constant quest to understand a patient's journey across the continuum of care, health-care providers are eyeing big data technologies to drive the patient life cycle, from an initial physician encounter and diagnosis through rehabilitation and follow-up. Such life-cycle management capabilities include structured and unstructured big data—social media interactions, physician notes, radiology images, and pharmacy prescriptions among them—that can populate and enrich a patient's health record. This data can then be stored in Hadoop, repopulated into the operational systems, or prepared for subsequent analytics via a data warehouse or mart.

Figure 5-3 illustrates a simple big data technology environment with Hadoop at the center of the data storage and processing environment. It might be typical of a small big data start-up because it assumes no legacy technology environment for managing small volumes of structured data.

Note that in the example the data sources themselves are heterogeneous, involving more diverse unstructured and semistructured data sets like e-mails, web server logs, or images. These data sources are increasingly likely to be found outside of the company's firewall as external data. Companies adopting production-class big data environments need faster and lower-cost ways to process large amounts of

FIGURE 5-3

A big data technology ecosystem

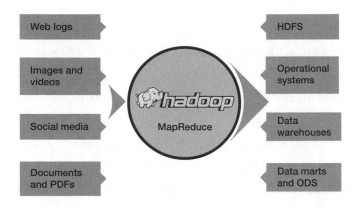

Source: SAS Best Practices.

atypical data. Think of the computing horsepower needed by energy companies to process data streaming from smart meters, or by retailers tracking in-store smartphone navigation paths, or LinkedIn's reconciliation of millions of colleague recommendations.

Or consider a gaming software company's ability to connect consumers with their friends via online video games. "Before big data, our legacy architecture was fairly typical," an executive explained in an interview. "Like most companies, we had data warehouses and lots of ETL programs and our data was very latent. And that meant that our analytics were very reactive." The gaming company revamped not only its analytics technology stack, but the guiding principles on which it processed its data, stressing business relevance and scalability. The IT group adopted Hadoop and began using advanced analytical algorithms to drive better prediction, thus optimizing customer offers and pricing. The gaming executive explained: "Once we were able to really exploit big data technology, we could then focus on the gamer's overall persona. This allowed all the data around the gamer to be more accurate, giving us a single identity connecting the gamer to the games, her friends, the games her friends are playing, her payment and purchase history, and her play preferences. The data is the glue that connects everything."[4]

Hadoop offers these companies a way to not only ingest the data quickly, but to process and store it for re-use. Because of its superior price performance, some companies are even betting on Hadoop as a data warehouse replacement, in some cases also using familiar SQL query languages in order to make big data more consumable for business users. Then again, many big companies have already invested millions in incumbent analytics environments like EDWs and have no plans on replacing them anytime soon.

What Most Large Companies Do Today

The classic analytics environment at most big companies includes the operational systems that serve as the sources for data; a data warehouse or collection of federated data marts that house and—ideally—integrate the data for a range of analysis functions; and a set of business intelligence and analytics tools that enable decisions from the use of ad hoc queries, dashboards, and data mining. Figure 5-4 illustrates the typical big company data warehouse ecosystem.

Indeed, big companies have invested tens of millions of dollars in hardware platforms, databases, ETL (extract, transform, and load) software, BI (business intelligence) dashboards, advanced analytics tools, maintenance contracts, upgrades, middleware, and storage systems that comprise robust, enterprise-class data warehouse environments.

In the best cases, these environments have helped companies understand their customer purchase and behavior patterns across channels and relationships, streamline sales processes, optimize

FIGURE 5-4

A typical data warehouse environment

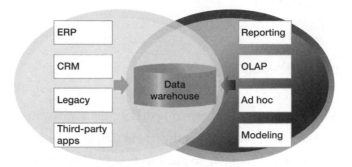

Source: SAS Best Practices.

product pricing and packaging, and drive more relevant conversations with prospects, thereby enhancing their brands. In the worst cases, companies have overinvested in these technologies, with many unable to recoup their investments in analytics and having to view their data warehouse infrastructures as sunk costs with marginal business value.

The more mature a company's analytics environment, the more likely it is that it represents a combination of historical successes and failures. In some cases, EDWs have become victims of their own success, serving as a popular, accessible repository not only for data to be analyzed, but also data in production transaction systems. Organizations using EDWs this way may embrace big data tools as a way to offload some of the jumbled data in their warehouses. While it seems unlikely that Hadoop and other big data technologies will replace data warehouses altogether, they will play a significant role in augmenting the choices organizations can make.

Best practice organizations approach BI and analytics not as a single project focused on a centralized platform, but as a series of business capabilities deployed over time, exploiting a common infrastructure and reusable data. Big data introduces fresh opportunities to expand this vision and deploy new capabilities that incumbent systems aren't optimized to handle.

Putting the Pieces Together

Big companies with large investments in their data warehouses generally have neither the resources nor the will to simply replace an environment that works well doing what it was designed to do. At the majority of big companies, a coexistence strategy that combines the best of legacy data warehouse and analytics environments with the new power of big data solutions is the best of both worlds, as shown in figure 5-5.

Many companies continue to rely on incumbent data warehouses for standard BI and analytics reporting, including regional sales reports, customer dashboards, or credit risk history. In this new environment, the data warehouse can continue with its standard workload, using data from legacy operational systems and

FIGURE 5-5

Big data and data warehouse coexistence

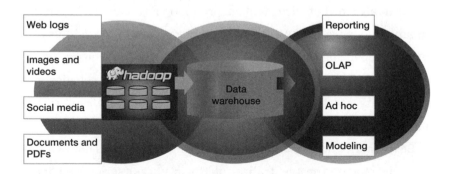

Source: SAS Best Practices.

storing historical data to provision traditional business intelligence and analytics results. But those operational systems can also populate the big data environment when they're needed for computation-rich processing or for raw data exploration. A company can steer the workload to the right platform based on what that platform was designed to do.

This coexistence of data environments minimizes disruption to existing analytics functions while at the same time accelerating new or strategic business processes that might benefit from increased speed. Figure 5-5 shows that the big data environment can serve as a data source for the enterprise data warehouse. As another possibility, Hadoop can serve as a staging and exploration area—what one company referred to as "the first stages in the information refining process"—for data that can eventually populate the data warehouse for subsequent analytics. Some organizations already use it as a first "preprocessing" step for data transformation, exploration, and discovery of patterns and trends, though there are other possibilities as well for this discovery platform, such as the Teradata Aster appliance.

There may well be other—and ultimately more complex—alternatives for data storage and processing in larger organizations. One big bank where I interviewed, for example, has four alternatives: a Hadoop cluster, a Teradata Aster big data appliance, a "light" data warehouse with few restrictions on how the data is managed, and a "heavy" EDW. Why so many, and what are the consequences of all these choices?

First and foremost, the bank has a large Teradata EDW. Like all such environments, it's not a quick and nimble place to put your data, particularly if the data is relatively unstructured. The rise of unstructured data types is poorly suited to the underlying relational data model on which almost all EDWs function. The ETL process for getting data out of transactional systems and into an EDW was always a bit burdensome, but with massive volumes of high-velocity data it becomes a real problem. However, the EDW is still the best place for putting production-level applications with an analytical focus—propensity scoring, real-time fraud detection, and so on.

The bank also has some smaller Teradata warehouses (informally called "Teradata lite") for which the process for getting data in and out is a bit less structured. These warehouses are typically much smaller and more focused—verging on the "mart" classification—and the data is less sensitive and permanent. So those are two alternatives for storing data that is destined to be analyzed.

What's next in the alternative platform list? The bank, like many other firms, likes the price and performance of Hadoop clusters, so it invested in one. The result is a fast, cheap tool for exploring and storing data and doing rudimentary analysis on it. However, the Hadoop platform has little security, backup, version control, or other data management hygiene functions, so it's suited only for data exploration and short-term storage of nonessential, nonsecure data. And working with it requires those data scientist–like skills involving Hadoop and MapReduce, and knowledge of scripting languages. The bank's data managers wonder if the cost of those skills outweighs the savings on the hardware and software for this platform, but there hasn't been a formal accounting yet.

But the bank acquired another platform for big data exploration from Teradata Aster. It's a platform that allows quick processing of data—for example, "sessionizing" customer interactions through the online banking site—and some analytical functions. The bank likes the fact that analysts can write queries in SQL for this platform without having to learn new and expensive skills.

So each of the four platforms has its niche. Some are intended as long-term homes for data, others for short residencies. Some are for exploration, others for production. Some allow considerable analytical work within the platform, others require going outside of it. The bank is in the process of creating a clear process for deciding what data goes where. It is happy to have all these options for data management platforms; however, it's undeniable that the current environment at this bank is much more complex than what prevailed in the past. And it is probably going to become more complex before it gets simplified.

By the end of 2013, there will be more mobile devices than people on the planet.[5] This will create both massive opportunity and massive complexity. Harnessing data from a range of new technology sources gives companies a richer understanding of consumer behaviors and preferences—irrespective of whether those consumers are existing or future customers. Big data technologies not only scale to larger data volumes more cost effectively, they support a range of new data and device types. The flexibility of these technologies is only as limited as the organization's vision.

By circumscribing a specific set of business problems, companies considering big data can be more specific about the corresponding functional capabilities and the big data projects or service providers that can help address them. This approach can inform both the acquisition of new big data technologies and the re-architecting of existing ones to fit into the brave new world of big data.

ACTION PLAN FOR MANAGERS

Technology for Big Data

- If you're not in the IT function, have you had a discussion with that group about how to add big data capabilities to your existing IT architecture?

- Have you identified the initial business problems that you think new big data technologies can help you with?

- Have you focused on the set of existing technologies that will continue to play a role in your organization?

- Do you have the right technology architecture and implementation skills in place to develop or customize big data solutions to fit your needs?

- Do these new solutions need to "talk to" your incumbent platforms? If so, how are you going to enable that? Are there open-source projects and tools that can give you a head start?

- Assuming that it's not practical for you to acquire all the big data-enabling technologies you need in one fell swoop, can you establish acquisition tiers for key big data solutions and the corresponding budget resources for each tier?

What It Takes to Succeed with Big Data

I n this chapter, I describe what it takes to succeed with big data in addition to technology. I have touched on some of these issues in other chapters, but here I will give a more comprehensive perspective. Since chapters 7 and 8 are about big data in small (and online) and big companies, respectively, I won't presume any particular size of organization in this one.

DELTA Revisited

Several years ago, I developed the DELTA (*d*ata, *e*nterprise, *l*eadership, *t*argets, and *a*nalysts) model for how to build analytical capabilities within an organization. I'm happy to say that it has been used by a number of organizations over the past several years. It is also the basis for an assessment tool used by the International Institute for Analytics (an organization I cofounded several years ago). I have

FIGURE 6-1

The DELTA model for traditional analytics and big data

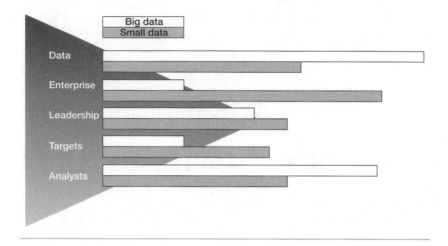

modified that assessment model to address big data, and it's included in the appendix. Since the DELTA model is described in some detail in the book *Analytics at Work*, I won't elaborate on it here as it applies to traditional analytics. However, it may be useful to contrast the five factors in the model across big data and traditional analytics.

For one difference, the factors show different levels of emphasis for big data (figure 6-1). In the following section, I'll describe how and why the emphasis differs, and what the focus is for big data in that factor.

Data for Big Data

Data itself is, of course, one of the most important factors overall in whether big data initiatives succeed. As figure 6-1 suggests, data in the big data context receives considerably more attention than it did in the small data, traditional analytics work. Needless to say, if you don't have data, you will have a tough time with big data. In addition to being part of the name of the phenomenon, data is important to big data because a major focus of effort is capturing, processing, and structuring data so that it can be analyzed.

Most of the data-related efforts in big data projects involve the work done prior to analysis: identifying possible sources of data, processing to transform unstructured data into structured, and integrating multiple sources of data into a common data set. Many organizations refer to these as the primary activities in data science. These activities—with the exception of data integration—are less common with traditional analytics. Some activities, such as identifying new and proprietary types of data, are equally important in both domains. Finally, there are some data management activities that are more advanced in the traditional analytics sphere than in big data.

As yet, most organizations pursuing big data have not yet engaged in extensive traditional data management efforts (including governance, as I mentioned in chapter 5). However, a few leading firms are beginning to combine data science activities with traditional data management virtues. Solid knowledge of data architectures, metadata, data quality and correction processes, data stewardship and administration dashboards, master data management hubs, matching algorithms, and a host of other data-specific topics are important for firms pursuing big data as a long-term strategic differentiator. The most governance-conscious firms will develop governance approaches that cut across all data types. The insurance company USAA—a company with a long history of leading-edge work in IT more generally—is clearly one of those firms. Tim Riley, USAA's information architect, commented in an interview: "We're building data governance into our big data processes. We're adding metadata and assigning data classification levels to understand usage and consumption. We're dealing with new types of data we haven't dealt with before. And we're calling out the features and meta-content that needs to be captured along the way." And Shannon Gilbert, executive director of BI Delivery and Governance, noted, "Our data governance efforts will pervade our environment. It applies to our data warehouses, our marts, and even our operational systems. After all, we consider data a corporate asset—and we treat it that way, no matter what the application."[1]

While such governance efforts undeniably represent sound practice, some on the business side (as opposed to IT) may be less interested in these data management capabilities, and in fact I have heard complaints (though not at USAA) when IT groups tried to impose them. One banking technologist said that his bank was pursuing ways to explore big data much more rapidly, then commented ruefully, "Then we give it to IT and they slow things down dramatically." Data governance, security, and reliability will continue to be issues on which impatient data scientists and big data advocates conflict with IT.

I have typically included analytical technology in the *data* category of the DELTA model. However, in the big data environment, technology is an important enough resource to deserve its own letter. I've already discussed it in chapter 5, so I won't do so again here. However, if you plan to use the DELTA model to assess and improve your big data capabilities, you might want to modify it to read DELTTA (the additional *T* for *technology*). That's the version I have used in the appendix.

Enterprise Orientation for Big Data

In traditional analytics, it's important to take an enterprise focus—to share data, technology, and people across the organization to achieve your analytical objectives. But for the early adopters of big data—primarily start-ups and online firms—this wasn't much of an issue. People were anxious simply to get something going, and how it related to other big data and analytics initiatives was not much of a concern.

That situation still prevails to some degree in large organizations that have adopted big data programs, as they are usually in the early stages—still doing proofs of concept or data discovery as opposed to full production applications—and rationalizing resources or creating synergies across projects will come later.

However, as I will discuss in detail in chapter 8, there is one factor that is leading to more enterprise coordination: the integration of big data and traditional analytics in large organizations. I interviewed with twenty large organizations pursuing big data initiatives, and not a single one was dealing with big data separately from traditional analytics. The same organizations and people were addressing both topics using a combined set of technologies. This is a good thing, I believe; creating parallel capabilities would lead to both overlaps and confusion.

But despite the fact that big data and traditional analytics are often combined in large companies, a high level of coordination of big data projects across the enterprise is somewhat unusual at this point. Most organizations that are not in online business typically have only one or two big data projects anyway, so there isn't yet a strong need for coordination. In the future, perhaps, we will see companies pursuing multiple big data initiatives across different functions and units, and they will feel a greater need to coordinate those initiatives, as they have done with traditional analytics programs. At the moment, however, this is not a primary concern.

Leadership for Big Data

Leadership is a critical factor in the success of traditional analytics programs, and it's just as important for big data. We don't have a lot of examples of leaders of companies with substantial commitments to big data, so I've given small data settings a slight lead on this factor in figure 6-1. However, we can begin to make some generalizations about the approaches followed by these relatively few big data leaders. They differ at least slightly from leaders of traditional analytical competitors.

One key leadership trait for big data seems to be a willingness to sponsor experimental activity with data on a large scale. Big data, at least today, requires some educated faith. ROI is difficult to define in advance—particularly when it involves new products and services or faster decisions. This is especially true in the discovery phase. As Tasso Argyros, cofounder of Aster Data (now Teradata Aster) notes, "It's rare that there is a budget for discovery."[2]

There are some leaders who are willing to venture into big data on faith, however. At LinkedIn, for example, cofounder Reid Hoffman had also been a founder of PayPal, and knew there were substantial opportunities from exploiting online transaction data. It was primarily his decision to begin hiring data scientists into the product engineering organization. He encouraged them not only to try to develop new products and services, but also to contact him directly if their ideas got stuck in the process or the hierarchy.

That's exactly what Jonathan Goldman, a data scientist at LinkedIn whom Hoffman had helped recruit, did when he had an idea for a new application that became People You May Know (PYMK).[3] The application recommends people you may want to network with who have background attributes in common with you. Goldman created an early prototype of PYMK, but had difficulty getting the product engineering organization to incorporate it into the LinkedIn site—or even to try it.

After Goldman approached Hoffman with his problem, Hoffman allowed him to create a test ad on the LinkedIn site. The click-through rate on those ads was the highest ever seen. Goldman continued to refine how the suggestions were generated, incorporating networking ideas such as *triangle closing*—the notion that if you know Larry and Sue, there's a good chance that Larry and Sue know each other. Goldman and his team also got the action required to respond to a suggestion down to one click.

LinkedIn's top managers quickly made PYMK a standard feature. That's when things really took off. I've already mentioned in chapter 1 that PYMK messages achieved a click-through rate 30 percent higher than the rate obtained by other prompts to get people to return to the site. Millions of people paid repeat visits who would not have done so otherwise. Thanks to this one feature, LinkedIn's growth trajectory shifted significantly upward; PYMK is credited with bringing in several million new users. It wouldn't have happened without Goldman's idea—and Hoffman's support of it.

It won't always be necessary for data scientists to go directly to the company's chairman, but it's not a bad idea for senior executives to open a direct channel to them in the early days of the big data era. Part of taking an interest in experimentation is eliminating barriers to the implementation of innovative ideas and offerings.

Leaders of big data–intensive organizations also need some degree of patience. A good deal of "mucking around in data" may be necessary before there is any sense of a payoff. It may even be necessary to keep data around for multiple years before its value is known. Jeff Bezos of Amazon is known for saying, "We never throw away data," simply because it is difficult to know when it may become important for a product or service offering down the road.

Leadership of big data firms may also require some new senior management roles. There are no examples—to my knowledge, anyway—of "Senior Vice Presidents of Big Data," but there are some roles that include that function. Take, for example, Nora Denzel, who was the senior vice president not only of marketing, but also of big data and social design at Intuit (and *big data* actually comes first—her official title there was Senior Vice President of Big Data, Social Design and

Marketing). There is a logic to combining these roles; at Intuit, big data is used to improve the website, build customer loyalty, and improve customer satisfaction—all marketing objectives.

Intuit has a great track record of developing products, services, and features based on big data. In the tax processing application TurboTax, for example, users are informed about how likely their tax returns are to be audited based on past customer experience. In the accounting package Quickbooks, products that customers buy and list in their financial records are the basis for targeted offers (called Easy Saver) of discounts on those products. Both Quickbooks and Mint, the personal finance site purchased by Intuit, inform business owners how their performance measures and costs relate to other small businesses.[4]

There are also new senior management roles at other firms involving the combination of big data and analytics. The insurance giant AIG, for example, brought in long-term analytics leader Murli Buluswar to be chief science officer—one of a growing number of C-level analytics executives in large firms. Buluswar oversees a variety of analytical projects and groups, involving both big data and small. His staff includes data scientists and conventional quantitative analysts. He commented in an interview: "From the beginning of our science function at AIG, our focus was on both traditional analytics and big data. We make use of structured and unstructured data, open-source and traditional analytics tools. We're working on traditional insurance analytics issues like pricing optimization, and some exotic big data problems in collaboration with MIT. It was and will continue to be an integrated approach."[5]

We're already beginning to see more roles of this type, with a variety of specific titles. One variation is the chief data officer (CDO) role, which is pretty common in large banks. In principle, I think it is a fine idea to combine the responsibility for data management and governance with the application of data—that is, analytics. In practice, however, most of the CDO incumbents seem to spend the great majority of their time on data management and not much on analytics. Most of them don't have strong analytics backgrounds either.

There are some exceptions, of course. John Carter was the CDO at Equifax, where he led efforts to build the company's analytical capabilities—while still wrestling with many data management issues as well. And Carter has a PhD in statistics. Now, however, he has a different job at Charles Schwab. He is Senior Vice President of Analytics, Insight, and Loyalty, which should allow more of a focus on what the company should do with big data.

There is another new analytics-intensive role at eBay. Zoher Karu, who led analytics efforts at Sears, will be the new vice president of customer optimization and data. Karu told me that the job was initially described in terms of customer analytics, but he felt that the term "optimization" suggests a stronger focus on achieving results.[6] Other companies, such as McGraw-Hill, are creating chief digital officers to both advocate for big data and analytics and manage online channels. Bank of America and Wells Fargo also combine those roles, although they don't employ the title.

Then there are the C-level titles that are purely focused on analytics. FICO, the University of Pittsburgh Medical Center, and the Obama 2012 campaign are three organizations that have named chief analytics officers. If you are really serious about analytics—not just the data management activities required for big data—and you want to employ them in a variety of functions and units around your organization, I recommend the creation of this sort of job and title.

Targets for Big Data

Targets means that organizations need to select where they are going to apply big data and analytics within their businesses. At a high level, will the resource be applied to supply chain decisions, customer decisions, financial decisions, human resource decisions, or some other area? And once an organization has prioritized, say, customer decisions, it then has to prioritize among segmenting customers by type, creating better targeted customer offers, identifying customers likely to attrite or leave, rewarding the most loyal customers, and so forth. One cannot simply do everything with analytics at once, so targeting choices is a necessary process.

However, targeting has been more of a focus for conventional analytics than for big data in the short history of their coexistence. With big data projects, many organizations are just trying something to see if it will work; they are at the proof-of-concept stage. The projects are often picked because they are convenient or because the owners or stakeholders are willing to experiment. Rarely do organizations make a concerted attempt to determine what the most important or strategic project would be before beginning work on something.

Despite this lack of attention to targets thus far, it's clear that an organization can't deal with all big data at once, nor apply it all at once to all the areas of the business that might benefit from it. Targeting, then, is a necessary activity. Your management team needs to come up with answers to some of the following questions:

- Where do we have significant data resources that are unexploited?

- Which of our business processes is most in need of better decision making?

- Where would we benefit from much faster decision making?

- Are we processing large amounts of data that would benefit in terms of cost reduction from big data technology?

- How might we create data-based products or services, and in which parts of our business would they be most relevant and useful?

- Is someone else in our industry likely to employ big data in a way that will disadvantage us? If so, how are they likely to use it?

Since the exploitation of big data can involve new products and services (in addition to internal decision support), there may well need to be more integration of big data initiative targeting with product development and strategy processes. If you're developing a new product, can there be a big data adjunct to it—perhaps in the form of a service? If you're thinking about disruptive innovations in your industry, how might big data contribute to them?

Analysts for Big Data

I have largely covered this topic in chapter 4, where I discussed the human side of big data. The only issue to address here is whether smart human analysts are any more important with big data than they were with traditional analytics. There is probably more emphasis on data scientists in big data than there was on quantitative analysts for analytics in the "old days." But that's not because they're more important; they're just harder to find, and they have a sexy new job title. The combination of technical and analytical skills required to be a successful data scientist makes them, as I noted in chapter 4, somewhat rare and difficult to recruit. Otherwise, you'll need smart, capable people to do business analytics, regardless of what type of data you are employing. If you're building your business around big data and analytics, like

Google, GE, LinkedIn, and other household names I have mentioned often in this book, you'll need hundreds of them.

Other Factors to Consider in Big Data Success

When I was coauthoring (with Jeanne Harris and Bob Morison) *Analytics at Work,* my initial idea was to describe not only the DELTA model, but also the FORCE model—which made not only for a somewhat silly combined set of acronyms, but also an overly complex approach to building (and in particular, maintaining) analytical capability. Just for the historical record, FORCE stood for:

- *Fact-based* decision making

- *Organization* of analysts and other resources

- Continual *review* of business assumptions and analytical models

- Reinforcing *culture* of analytical decisions and "test and learn"

- *Embedding* analytics in major business processes

All of these factors are also important to big data, but many of them are discussed elsewhere in this book. So in this section I'll consider only two of the letters—C (culture), and E (embedding analytics—and big data—in major business processes). We did end up writing chapters on those topics in *Analytics at Work,* so I will refer you to that book for comments on them with regard to traditional analytics. The following sections relate to some special issues for big data.

Culture

Is there a big data culture? Or put more precisely, is a big data culture different from an analytics-oriented culture? The differences
are subtle, and a firm that wants to succeed with big data could do
much worse than to adopt a culture that emphasizes analytical and
fact-based decisions. However, here are some of the attributes of a big
data culture that I've observed.

> *Impatience with the status quo, and a sense of urgency:* This
> trait is common among successful organizations of any size or
> type, but it's particularly pronounced among the start-up big
> data firms. Among the data scientists and company leaders I
> interviewed, there was a strong belief that the big data market is
> a land grab, and to the early movers will go the spoils. One impli-
> cation is that these impatient individuals will move on quickly if
> their current employer isn't moving quickly enough.

> *A strong focus on innovation and exploration:* Big data firms are
> constantly innovating, exploring, and experimenting to learn
> more about their operations and their customers. Google was
> perhaps the first big data firm, and it sets the tone for culture. It
> encourages every employee to be innovative and gives engineers
> a percentage of their time to work on new products. According
> to Google's chief economist Hal Varian, the company carries out
> about ten thousand controlled experiments a year—roughly half
> on search-related innovations and half on advertising. Google even
> tries to get advertisers (through a program called Advertiser Cam-
> paign Experiments) and publishers to do more experimentation.

> *Belief in technology as a source of disruption:* For many early
> adopters of big data, technological innovation is as important
> as data innovation. Firms like Google, Yahoo!, and Facebook

encouraged their data scientists to develop new tools and even to make them available as open-source projects (MapReduce, Hadoop, Pig, and Hive originally came out of these companies). Google and Amazon push the frontiers of not only software, but also hardware and data center technologies. LinkedIn's data scientists argue that they have benefitted from open-source technologies themselves, so they are making some of their own technologies available as open-source projects too. It's likely that early adopters of big data will have to continue with technological innovation, and at least some of them will share them with the outside world. I'll describe this attribute of big data start-ups and online firms further in chapter 7.

A culture of commitment: The leaders in big data are willing to commit to bold, audacious goals—and they are particularly audacious at this early stage for big data in large organizations. Google committed to making the self-driving car a reality—a project it considers to be based on big data. GE's management team and board of directors were willing to commit a couple of billion dollars to building its capabilities in software and big data. Even for a very large company like GE, that's a major commitment. If your company hasn't even discussed big data at the senior management or board level, you may want to address that situation.

Nonhierarchical and meritocratic organization: Big data early adopters believe that big ideas can come from anywhere and anyone in the organization. LinkedIn, one of the most successful firms at creating new products and services with big data, was cofounded by Reid Hoffman. I've already discussed how he empowered Jonathan Goldman to develop the People You May Know feature.

This sort of meritocratic empowerment is a personal philosophy of Hoffman's: "I want to enable individual professionals to have more successful careers and to increase the productivity of mankind across entire industries and countries. I want a company that lives up to the original standard that Hewlett-Packard set for Silicon Valley—a great place for high-quality people to work that provides an experience that would continue to benefit them even after they move on to other things."[7]

Of course, it's still early days for talking about the culture of big data organizations—and every other attribute of them, for that matter. And some executives may feel that changing the culture, leadership, or other approaches within their organizations merely to facilitate big data initiatives would be the tail wagging the dog. I'd argue, however, that this business resource is significant enough to be worthy of such changes. And most of them bring along other benefits (in addition to being more big data-friendly) as well!

Embedding Big Data

The other FORCE word I'd like to describe here is *embedding*— referring to embedding big data, and the analytics based on big data, into key operational and decision processes. I'm not talking about fully robotic (machine-only) processes—humans can still review and override the recommended actions from such automated systems— but it is important to employ automation to ensure that analytics and big data are employed in a timely and efficient fashion.

As big data and analyses based on it proliferate in society and organizations, we simply won't have the time or the human labor to present those results to humans for decision making. And we know more and more about the irrational decision processes that many humans employ; why wouldn't we prefer more automated analytical decisions in many cases?

Analytics in the small data era were just beginning to become more automated when big data came along. Now we have no choice but to embed big data–based analyses into business processes. Some analysts refer to this as *smart BPM* (business process management); others, such as James Taylor, are advocates of the term *enterprise decision management*. Regardless of what we call it, it needs to happen more in the future. It's already true in many aspects of the financial services industry, but it needs to move into many other industries as well.[8]

Take, for example, an application that manages arrivals and departures at Heathrow Airport, created by Heathrow Airport Holdings, previously known as the British Airport Authority.[9] The airport gets 65 million passengers a year and runs at 98 percent runway capacity for its thirteen hundred flights per day, so making good decisions rapidly about what to do with arriving and departing planes is critical to its success. Shortening taxi times, for example, can save up to thirty thousand tons of carbon dioxide emissions per year.

Heathrow has been implementing a semiautomated system for managing flight operations—called Airport Collaborative Decision Making (A-CDM) for several years. Using a set of decision rules and process flows, this system automatically creates and dynamically coordinates all operations involved in flight turnaround, including exactly when a plane will land, which gate it should taxi to, how much baggage needs to be offloaded, when refueling will happen, the arrival time of the next flight crew, the time passengers will board, and when the plane should push back and take off. Working with smart BPM vendor Pegasystems, Heathrow completed the first phase of the system in a little over two months, and immediately improved the percentage of on-time departures from 60 to 85 percent.

The decision rules are increasingly being complemented by predictive and optimization models to improve the operational performance of the system and the airport. Heathrow's system has also been linked with other airports in the European network, so that it can get more data about plane arrivals and departures. Now, with big data upon us, the system also increasingly includes data from sensors in the runways, on airplanes, and on vehicles like fuel trucks and baggage carts. It would simply be impossible for humans to deal with all of this data without an automated process.

It's clear, then, that the stand-alone era for big data and analytics is approaching the end of its useful life. Increasingly, a computer, not a human (or humans), will be receiving the output of a big data analysis. That computer will generate instructions for not only people but other machines, which will then generate more data on their operations and performance. Will the last human being to leave the big data building please turn out the lights?

ACTION PLAN FOR MANAGERS

What It Takes to Succeed with Big Data

- Do you have an impressive collection of data on key business topics that you can exploit?

- Are you starting to coordinate big data and analytics projects across the enterprise?

- Are you and your fellow executives providing strong, passionate leadership for big data and analytics?

- Have you identified a set of targets for your big data work going forward?

- Do you have the data scientists and analysts you need?

- Is your culture supportive of making decisions on the basis of big data and creating new products and services based on it?

- Are you beginning to embed big data analyses into automated systems and processes?

7

What You Can Learn from Start-Ups and Online Firms

Much of the earliest big data activity was in firms with online products and services—Google, eBay, Yahoo!, Facebook, LinkedIn, and the other usual suspects and start-ups in online and related sectors. We owe these organizations a considerable debt because they established the function of data science and other disciplines of big data. In this chapter, I'll reflect on the many lessons we can learn from these early adopters. Not all of them may be useful in, for example, a large bank, but they should at least be considered. And if you work in a large bank, don't worry, you are not being ignored—chapter 8 is about the application of big data to big companies just like yours. To provide greater context about what is happening with big data in the small and large firms I've researched, I've developed a set of short case studies that are spread throughout the two chapters.

Start-up and online firms had something of a clean slate relative to big data. Since most of these companies were new and in the data business from the beginning, they didn't have to worry much about how to integrate big data with smaller, structured data types. They may have established a conventional information infrastructure for internal applications like general ledger and payroll, but they didn't spend a lot of time or attention on it. Their focus was almost exclusively on big data, and it was generally the focus of engineering or product development organizations rather than the IT function. Some of the smaller start-up firms don't even have in-house IT functions; they outsource business IT.

Some of the big data lessons from start-up and online firms are derived from and are similar to other general IT and entrepreneurship lessons from Silicon Valley firms. They include the injunction, popularized by Facebook founder Mark Zuckerberg, to "move fast and break things," and not worry too much about making mistakes. Another is to have bold and audacious goals that involve objectives other than simply making a lot of money. Facebook hopes to "make the world more open and connected." Google's well-publicized mission is to "organize the world's information and make it universally accessible and useful." However, these general lessons have only limited relevance to big data topics, and they are pretty well known in the business literature. Therefore, I won't address them further in this chapter.

Lessons from Big Data Start-Ups and Online Firms

Since big data start-ups and larger online firms originated the idea of "data products" based on their own data and analytics, there are many positive lessons that other organizations can learn from such companies.

Use Big Data for Product and Service Innovation

I noted in chapter 3 that one of the potential benefits of big data is developing new products or services for customers, but most of the actual examples of that benefit are found in online and start-up firms—Google, LinkedIn, Facebook, Amazon, and so forth. I believe that innovation is the highest and best use of big data, so firms in other industries should emulate the Silicon Valley companies. Devoting your big data efforts to product and service innovation may well be the most important lesson from these companies.

Of course, this is more difficult when your customer offerings are tangible goods rather than data. The "common" (though they are obviously still emerging) approaches to adding big data to products involve services—capturing and analyzing data on how the products are being used, when they are likely to break, and how they can be serviced most effectively and efficiently. It's also possible to use big data to inform customers about their behavior relative to a product—how to drive a car in a more energy-efficient manner, for example. Data can also be embedded in the product itself, as it is for the Tesla Model S. Vehicle data logs for the car can be used to monitor performance remotely, signal the need for maintenance, and let drivers know how their mileage and performance compare with other drivers' experience.

Taking advantage of this lesson can be difficult if your primary business doesn't involve big data or related technologies. But there are several ways to get started if you are a large, not-so-nimble organization. One is to create a separate business unit for selling data, insights, and technology. That's what UnitedHealth Group did in 1996, when it created Ingenix (now Optum), a business based on selling data, insights, and software to health-care companies. The company has grown organically, and many acquisitions have been integrated into Optum. The unit's annual revenues are now over $25 billion. Having

Optum as part of the UnitedHealth family has been very beneficial in an industry such as health care that is in the midst of a revolution based on analytics and big data.

Another approach to getting started is to acquire start-ups or smaller firms that specialize in using and selling big data. Again in health care, that approach has been taken by Humana, which bought Anvita Health in 2011. Anvita supplies clinical analytics and software to health-care organizations; Humana was originally one of its customers. Now Humana is integrating Anvita's offerings into a broader set of analytics and big data capabilities.

A third option for jumping into big data businesses is to partner. An example, again in the health-care industry, is the approach taken by Intermountain Healthcare, a Salt Lake City–based health-care provider with twenty-two hospitals and two hundred clinics that has built a reputation for analytically determined care processes. In 2011, the organization created the Homer Warner Center for Informatics Research, named after a pioneer in creating electronic health records at Intermountain. Then, in 2013, Intermountain partnered with Deloitte to offer services and solutions to other health-care organizations. Since Intermountain had forty years of data and more than two trillion data elements from its electronic health records, its partnership with Deloitte will help other providers identify optimal treatments for various health conditions.

Work on Tools, Not Just Applications

The earliest big data firms developed not only analytical applications, products, and features but also tools. The tools to divide up very large databases across multiple commodity servers simply didn't exist, so these firms had to create them. Fortunately, in many cases they also made them available to other firms (see the following). Google developed the MapReduce framework and published it in a 2004 paper by Jeffrey Dean and Sanjay Ghemawat.[1] Hadoop was developed by Doug Cutting of Yahoo! and Mike Cafarella, a professor at the University of Michigan. The scripting language Pig was also developed at Yahoo! in 2006, and the batch-oriented data-storage language Hive was developed at Facebook. Most of these firms are extremely successful, so there is no evidence that their tool development has hurt their performance (Yahoo! may be an exception, although it appears to be turning itself around).

Why would these companies work on tools? Because they had to. If they wanted to process and analyze their vast amounts of real-time data at a reasonable cost, they needed to develop new tools to do so. Today, of course, there are many more big data tools available. Do companies still need to develop them? Perhaps not at the basic infrastructural level, particularly given that many vendors have entered this space. Arguably, the world doesn't need another new version of Hadoop.

However, there will still be a need for tools that deal with particular types of idiosyncratic data. If you are trying to manage, for example, sensor data from refrigerators, chances are good that the data will have some unique features, and data management will probably require some special software to extract and manipulate it.

Give Data Scientists Their Heads

Big data start-ups tend to give lots of responsibility to data scientists. In some cases (e.g., the Bay Area firm Quid, and the Cambridge, Massachusetts, firm Recorded Future), the CEOs are data scientists themselves. In others, the data scientists get lots of responsibility for bringing new products and services to the market. Even in some large online firms, such as LinkedIn, they have a direct channel to senior management (see the case study "Big Data at LinkedIn").

This level of access and autonomy is obviously more difficult in a large company with thousands of people. If you have that situation, try to ensure that some senior executive in the company is responsible for ensuring that data scientists are listened to, and that their work is making a difference. Some organizations have begun to add digitally oriented executives to their boards of directors. This step makes sense for helping companies to understand big data, but it is unlikely to provide much aid and comfort to data scientist employees.

Big Data at LinkedIn

LinkedIn, founded in late 2002, has over 225 million members. It has become the go-to site for business networking around the world. There are many factors that contributed to LinkedIn's success, but big data is certainly one of them. There are big data activities taking place across the company, including in the Data Engineering team, the Data Products team, the Business Analytics team, and the Product Data Science Team. The term *data scientist* was first applied at LinkedIn, and the company has well over a hundred of them as employees.

I have mentioned more than once in this book the success that LinkedIn has had in developing new products and features (LinkedIn Skills, People You May Know, Talent Match, Similar Jobs, Groups You May Like, etc.), but there are many other domains of the company in which big data makes a contribution. LinkedIn recently developed a new set of *unified search* capabilities, for example, which use big data to predict the types of content a user is most likely to be interested in, and optimizing the presentation of results.

LinkedIn also employs big data for internal processes, including sales and marketing campaigns. For instance, LinkedIn has used some of its own internal data to predict which companies will buy LinkedIn products, and even who in those firms has the highest likelihood of buying. This work led to an internal recommendation system for salespeople that makes it much easier for them to get the data in one place, and has improved conversion rates by several hundred percent.

LinkedIn's cofounder, Reid Hoffman, is a strong advocate for big data:

> Because of Web 2.0 [the explosion of social networks and consumer participation in the web] and the increasing number of sensors, there's all this data. With these massive amounts of highly semantically indexed data that's indexed around people and places and all the things that matter to us and our lives, I believe there are going to be a ton of interesting apps that come out of that . . . the way our products and services are constituted, how we determine our strategy and maintain a competitive edge against other folks—if data is a very strong element of each of these, and you're not doing anything, it's like trying to run a business without business intelligence.[a]

a. E. B. Boyd, "LinkedIn's Reid Hoffman on Groupon's Big Advantage: Big Data," *FastCompany.com* blog post, http://www.fastcompany.com/1795868/linkedins-reid-hoffman-groupons-big-advantage-big-data.

Address the Productivity of Big Data Work

The best Silicon Valley firms have figured out that human productivity is the greatest constraint on big data advancement. It requires considerable activity by data scientists to extract data from where it resides, put it into a structured format suitable for analysis, and model and analyze it. And data scientist time is expensive time. So leading firms—again, primarily those in data-intensive online businesses—are taking steps to address the issue of data science productivity.

eBay was among the first to address data science productivity, creating a variety of tools and approaches to speed up data work. The company's managers created *virtual data marts*—data analysis environments that don't replicate existing data, but allow unique views and analysis of it—to ease the creation of data sets for analytics. A Data Hub was organized to facilitate sharing of data, algorithms, and insights. Teradata has created a product called Data Lab that is largely derived from the ideas at eBay, so other organizations can address the productivity issue as well. Another vendor, EMC Greenplum, has developed a set of tools called Pivotal Chorus that address data scientist productivity and collaboration.

LinkedIn is also working on data science productivity, creating an environment that allows automated website A/B testing (comparing whether one website design elicits more views or clicks than another). The company can conduct two thousand tests on any given day, and analyzing and interpreting the results is labor-intensive. So LinkedIn's data scientists spent a couple of months developing programs to analyze and report on A/B test results. The systems mimic what a data scientist or analyst would do relative to the tests. Within twenty-four hours of a test, they know the impact of it across up to four hundred different metrics.

Contribute to the Commons

Many of the products used for data science—Hadoop, Pig, Hive, Python—are open source, and they were contributed to the open-source community (specifically to The Apache Foundation) by the companies that developed them. There is a strong ethos of making tools broadly available to the big data community. As a group of researchers wrote about LinkedIn:

> LinkedIn contributes to the Voldemort distributed storage system and more than 10 more open-source projects. "We contribute,

they contribute and the code moves forward," says David Henke, senior vice president of operations at LinkedIn.[2]

Another LinkedIn data scientist told me:

> We are working on some database enhancements to a social graph database. They will be open source when we're done. There are some IP [intellectual property] considerations, but overall LinkedIn believes in building on the open-source framework since we benefit from it.

This lesson could be taken too far, of course. All of the companies I've mentioned keep some big data assets to themselves. However, given all the benefits that every firm has received from open-source software, virtually every firm should try to give something back.

Remember: Agile Is Too Slow!

Graham Gardner, the CEO of Kyruus, a Boston-based big data start-up in the health-care space, commented to me that, "We tried agile [a fast methodology for system development and project management], but it was too slow." Kyruus introduces new versions of its data and software almost daily (see the case study "Big Data at Kyruus"). And certainly when I interviewed about thirty data scientists in 2012, almost all of them were clearly impatient fast movers. One of the reasons the big data field has made such rapid progress is the impatience of its practitioners.

There is a downside to impatience, of course. It may mean that companies rush their products and services to market too quickly. This is a badge of honor in Silicon Valley—note LinkedIn cofounder and venture capitalist Reid Hoffman's comment, "If you are not embarrassed by your first release, you've launched too late!"—but it can result in offerings with as many bugs as features. It can also mean that data scientists move around a lot if they feel they are not accomplishing a lot quickly.

Big Data at Kyruus

Kyruus, founded in 2010 by Graham Gardner, a venture capitalist and physician, and Julie Yoo, a technology development manager, focuses on big data about physicians. It provides the data to hospitals, insurance firms, and pharmaceutical companies to help them better understand physician networks. Its goal was to become the "Bloomberg of physician information."

Kyruus began collecting its data from a variety of sources, including human resource databases, physician credentialing systems, electronic patient records, and supply chain databases—more than one thousand public and commercial sources. The company had several alternative sources of potential revenue from selling this data, but one became the most compelling. It involved tracking "leakage" of patient referrals outside of a hospital's care network. Gardner, the CEO, explained the importance of controlling leakage: "Some large health systems report upwards of 50% leakage from hospital networks, while best-in-class organizations have leakage rates of under 20% . . . If we were to change leakage rates by just a few percentage points, systems that were operating at a loss could become profitable."[a]

Kyruus is structured into three major groups: data acquisition, integration, and processing; analytics; and applications and the user interface. The company's data platform includes features to display and analyze data.

a. Robert F. Higgins, Penrose O'Donnell, and Mehul Bhatt, "Kyruus: Big Data's Search for the Killer App," Case 813-060 (Boston: Harvard Business School, 2012), 13.

Take Advantage of Free and Low-Cost Stuff

In the distant past—say, a decade ago—the costs of computing, data management, and data analysis were major impediments to big data (assuming you could find some in the first place). Today, however, start-ups and online firms make heavy use of inexpensive and free resources. The cloud is one; companies like Amazon (Elastic Compute Cloud, or Amazon EC2), Google (Compute Engine), and Microsoft (Windows Azure) make computing resources available at extremely low cost—or at least low capital expenditures—relative to the past. This is appealing to start-ups, which often have limited capital to invest. Cloud computing also has other benefits. As Christopher Ahlberg, the founder and CEO of big data start-up Recorded Future, describes the benefit of flexibility, "At the volume we use the cloud, it's actually pretty expensive. But the switching cost from one architecture to the next is dramatically lower—perhaps one or two orders of magnitude—so for anything that looks like a start-up that's a big breakthrough."[3]

I've already mentioned that start-ups and online firms also make extensive use of open-source software (in addition to making their proprietary software available as open source). They use not only data management tools like Hadoop, Pig, and Hive, but also open-source statistical software like R. As one data scientist said to me about R: "It's free, and it's what everybody coming out of school knows and wants to use. It's a no-brainer for us."

The primary downside to open-source computing for big data is that there may be less expensive solutions available when firms consider the cost of specialized resources—like data scientist labor. I asked Jim Davis, the head of marketing (among other functions) for analytical software firm SAS, what his thoughts were on competition from R.

He commented, "We don't see it very much. Most of our offerings are specialized solutions that help our customers do things like reduce credit card fraud in banking, or optimize revenue in travel. When customers find that there is already a solution to do what they need, they don't generally want to program it themselves in R."[4]

In general, I haven't seen much evidence that firms of any size have computed the total cost of ownership (TCO) for their big data technology. When and if they do, the appeal of open-source tools might be lessened somewhat.

Experiment on a Large Scale

One of the most powerful analytical approaches with big data is randomized, controlled experimentation, and it's done on a huge scale in online and start-up firms' websites.[5] This type of analysis is powerful because it's the only way to establish cause and effect. I've already mentioned A/B testing at LinkedIn—a technique involving running two different versions of a web page, randomly assigning customers to each, and then observing whether there are statistically significant differences in customer behavior across the pages.

Google and eBay also make extensive use of testing. Google's chief economist, Hal Varian, estimates that it does about ten thousand tests a year, half on search and half on advertising-related features. eBay is perhaps the most test-obsessed company I've ever come across. Not only does it do very extensive A/B testing and testing of alternative website designs, but it also conducts extensive offline tests, including lab studies, home visits, participatory design sessions, focus groups, and trade-off analysis of website features—all with customers. eBay also carries out quantitative visual-design research and eye-tracking studies, as well as diary studies, to see how users feel about potential changes.[6]

Online firms are pursuing two key directions in testing. One, as I mentioned with regard to LinkedIn, involves developing tools that automate aspects of the testing process. eBay, for example, has built the eBay Experimentation Platform, which leads testers through the process and keeps track of what's being tested at what times on what pages. LinkedIn has a similar capability, as I've mentioned. External vendors, such as Optimizely, also provide some of these capabilities for A/B testing of websites; a company called Applied Predictive Technologies offers software for the management of testing for offline tests.

The other key direction is to move beyond the incremental innovation that A/B testing often leads to. Normally, the A and B sites in an A/B test would differ only slightly; if you change more than one thing at once, it's impossible to know what is working. But firms like eBay and LinkedIn have approaches that involve making more dramatic changes in sites involving multiple changes at a time. More dramatic changes lead to more dramatic outcomes. LinkedIn, for example, can test more than twenty discrete changes to a page at one time. One change might create a 2 percent improvement in click-throughs; another might lead to a 5 percent reduction. If you combine twenty of them, the overall lift might be as high as 25 percent.

Foster Close Collaboration

When I interviewed senior data scientists in online and start-up firms in 2012, one of the questions I asked was how their organizations gathered all the necessary data science skills. Many said that they found it difficult to find the needed skills in a single individual, but had assembled teams that together had all the necessary skills. They often commented that the team members had to collaborate closely. When I asked how they did that—did they use any online collaboration tools, for example?—they almost always said that the necessary collaborations were easy because all the people involved were in one room! Many also use hackathons to create programming breakthroughs, which also typically take place in one room.

This sort of high-proximity, high-bandwidth communication can happen relatively easily in a small start-up firm with only a few employees. It is of course more difficult in a large firm. Google is well known for attempting to foster face-to-face collaboration in a large organization. It does so by:

- Putting at least two people in a cubicle

- Providing free high-quality meals to lure employees to the office

- Providing free transportation to the office

- Offering stimulating speakers and events in the office

- Making available a variety of spaces for informal "huddles"

The CEO of Yahoo!, Marissa Mayer, came from Google and was not pleased to find that a large number of Yahoo! employees worked from home. She quickly—and controversially—cancelled the home work policy and insisted that employees come into offices.[7] The memo announcing the new policy explained that face-to-face interactions foster a more collaborative culture. Mayer also instituted free cafeteria food and some other policies from Google.

It may seem ironic that these big data firms want collaboration through direct interaction rather than digital communication formats, but it seems to work for them. Organizations that have a variety of far-flung locations obviously need to find other means of fostering collaboration, but the objective is important in any case.

It's great that the online and start-up firms in Silicon Valley, Boston, and other big data hubs have been such a source of big data innovation.

Let's hope that all or most of these lessons make their way into larger and more traditional businesses. However, there are some examples of lessons not learned and things to avoid from start-up and online firms in the big data world, which is the subject of the next section.

Lessons Not Learned by Start-Ups and Online Firms

Although most of the big data lessons from online and start-up firms are very useful, these firms haven't always gotten it right. In some cases, they provide lessons for what not to do. These negative lessons may not lead to their downfall, and they don't apply to all firms. However, it's likely that by following these approaches, start-up firms are less successful than they could be.

Not Sharing Data with Customers

One of the more sensitive issues in big data is how much visibility customers have into data about or derived from their own online activities. Smart companies make that data available to their customers and allow them to use it for constructive purposes. One example would be to better understand the customer's use of the product or service the company provides.

Most online firms are not very good at letting you know what data they have about you, or sharing it with you for your own purposes. Facebook and Google regularly run afoul of customers, the press, and government regulators for lack of transparency with regard to customer information. Google will give you some information about your own search history and your use of its other products (in Google Dashboard), and it supplies reports on the user information it gives governments. But there is plenty that customers don't know.

Large firms have been the most progressive in this regard, although it's still early days for almost everyone. For example, San Diego Gas & Electric, through its "Green Button" program, supplies up to thirteen months of electricity usage data for customers wanting to analyze (and reduce) their own consumption.[8] The European mobile telecom firm Orange has a customer-centric data privacy policy, and has announced plans to let customers control their own usage data.

Collecting Data for Data's Sake

Some start-ups—and wealthy online firms like Amazon and Google—compile data for its own sake. They believe that they will eventually find uses for it. Google collects virtually every piece of data it can on its customers and their behavior, and sometimes it collects data when it shouldn't.[9] The Google StreetView mapping project that also collected unencrypted Wi-Fi data as it drove by is a prominent example. These firms have enough resources that they can afford to gather data without a purpose—though they might be even more successful if they thought about the purpose in advance of gathering the data.

Other start-ups in the big data space started with a pool of data, without having absolute clarity on what they were going to do with it. Kyruus is one example (see the previous case study); Recorded Future (see the case study "Big Data at Recorded Future") is another. This is less of a problem with start-ups, however, because they typically face pressure from investors to commit to a business model at an early stage. Both companies quickly found a focus for their product offerings and business models.

Big Data at Recorded Future

Christopher Ahlberg, the founder of Recorded Future (RF) and previously the founder of visual analytics firm Spotfire, was intrigued with the possibility of focusing visual and other forms of analytics on external information and in moving from descriptive to predictive analytics. For Ahlberg and RF (and for many other big data start-ups as well), there was no more obvious source of external information than the internet itself.

In 2009, Ahlberg teamed up with his Spotfire cofounders in Sweden to begin developing a "temporal analytics engine"—a set of quantitative and visual analysis tools to help analysts predict future events. RF made copies of large sections of the internet—including tens of thousands of websites, blogs, and Twitter accounts—for purposes of analysis. In total, it indexed over 8 billion events and entities, with their accompanying attributes (a web page, for example, might mention specific people, places, and activities that would align with a particular event or entity).

Using cloud-based computing, the RF tools not only count events and predictions, but also analyze sources to find "invisible links" between documents and pages that have some degree of relatedness. The goal of this analysis is to better understand the underlying events and entities and to determine the momentum or trends of the event discussion and to predict when they might happen. As at Spotfire, visual representations depict networks and temporal patterns in the past, present, and future.

RF has two basic offerings for its customers. For those who need software to analyze in-house data (primarily government intelligence agencies), it offers its Foresite platform, which provides tools for linguistic processing and scoring of events, entities, and time. The internet data itself—cleaned, indexed, and with a taxonomy for important terms—is the second primary offering. Intelligence agencies use RF to analyze trends and predictions involving terrorism, technology developments, and political unrest. Private-sector customers include corporate security departments, hedge funds, and companies wishing to track and analyze customer, competitor, and market intelligence.

As I argued in chapter 3, it's no crime to sift through a big pile of data to find out what gold nuggets might lie within it—in fact, it makes a lot of sense. However, sifting without a purpose can become very expensive and time-consuming. It's far better to have a hypothesis in mind—particularly before gathering a lot of data, and even before analyzing it.

One example of a focused big data start-up is Operating Analytics, a Boston-based firm that uses data and analytics to help hospitals optimize the use of their operating rooms. ORs are expensive resources, but their utilization varies widely within and across hospitals—and can dip below 50 percent. Optimizing OR use involves complex analyses involving rooms and specialized equipment in them, patients, doctor and staff availability, and outcome variables such as patient length of stay and readmission rates. The analysis is one that is difficult for hospitals to do themselves and for which a better solution will easily yield substantial revenue gains. It's still early days for Operating Analytics, but my sense is that a focused approach with a clear business problem and customer will always beat a big data fishing expedition.

Talking Too Much about Technology

The big data industry—particularly vendors of big data technology based in Silicon Valley, but sometimes other types of companies too—is greatly enamored of technology. Both internal discussions and materials, and the marketing materials these organizations produce for external consumption, are highly technological in nature, and difficult for non-techies to understand.

Many of these firms' websites toss around technical terms with abandon. Several tout "SQL-on-Hadoop" with little or no explanation of what it means or why it matters. One promises "Hadoop: Beyond Batch with Apache YARN," also with little elaboration on the purpose of YARN—but it is clearly "foundational to Hadoop 2.0."[10] Part of the problem is perhaps the names of the open-source projects that the Apache Foundation distributes: Apache Hadoop, Apache Flume, Apache HBase, Apache Mahout, Apache Oozie, Apache Zookeeper, and so on. I have been following big data for several years now, and I have never heard of Apache Oozie or Apache YARN. What must a non-technical business manager think of these terms?

Even IBM, which pioneered the business-oriented discussion of data processing many decades ago, sometimes succumbs to techno-speak. In its highest-level paragraph on "What Is Hadoop," for example, the short text includes the statement: "Rather than relying on high-end hardware, the resiliency of these clusters comes from the software's ability to detect and handle failures at the application layer."[11]

Sometimes it's necessary to use technical language, but in such cases there should be plenty of definitional material along with it. Most of the time, however, when we talk about big data we should talk about benefits, returns on investments, opportunities, and risks. Just as IBM learned (but seems to have forgotten) that lesson in selling other forms of information technology, it's time for big data vendors to learn it as well.

Focusing Too Much on Big Data Hype

Big data is all the rage, and venture capitalists are now succumbing to the big data gold rush—competing madly to fund start-ups in the space. One estimate in March 2013 of venture capital funding for only forty big data start-ups (and there are many more) came to $1.2 billion.[12] As is normal with that kind of money floating around, big entrepreneurs feel that they are in a land rush. Companies previously in analytics or software businesses are now in big data businesses. The worst managers rush offerings to market, promise more than they can deliver, and often dissatisfy customers.

That is not, of course, the route to long-term success. The big data movement is an important and long-lasting one, but it will evolve and change its name multiple times. What will matter is clearly defining your market and meeting the needs of your customers. As Raul Valdes-Perez, a former computer science professor and the founder of big data firm Vivisimo (which was acquired by IBM), noted about his company, "We used a blocking and tackling strategy—make a good product, explain it well, treat customers and prospects fairly, make skillful recruiting a top priority, and highlight our technology through well-chosen public demos and PR."[13]

———————————

Of course, the big data industry is still in its infancy. Some of these misjudgments may simply be the result of inexperience or immaturity. And what makes for success and failure in the industry will surely evolve over time. However, there have been previous generations of technology-based businesses before, and it's clear that ignoring good management practice has been a highly problematic approach no matter what the technology. That is surely the case with big data as well.

ACTION PLAN FOR MANAGERS

Learning about Big Data from Start-Ups and Online Firms

- Have you built aspects of your business model and products/ services partly around data and analytics?

- Have you devoted some of your data science efforts to tool development—and made the results available in the open-source community?

- Have you given your data scientists high levels of autonomy and responsibility?

- Have you tried to improve the productivity of your data science work?

- Have you accelerated your process for analysis and insight development?

- Do you have a culture and a process for widespread experimentation?

- Do you foster collaboration among your analysts and data scientists, and between them and their business partners?

- Have you avoided common mistakes of start-ups—not giving data to customers, collecting data for data's sake, talking too much about technology, and focusing too much on big data hype?

8

What You Can Learn from Large Companies

Big Data and Analytics 3.0

As I noted in chapter 7, the early adopters of big data in online and start-up firms were built around big data from the beginning. They didn't have to reconcile or integrate big data with more traditional sources of data and the analytics performed on them because they didn't have those traditional forms. They didn't have to merge big data technologies with their traditional IT infrastructures because those infrastructures didn't exist. Big data could stand alone, big data analytics could be the only focus of analytics, and big data technology architectures could be the only architecture.

Consider, however, the position of large, well-established businesses. Big data in those environments shouldn't be separate, but must be integrated with everything else that's going on. Analytics on big data have to coexist with analytics on other types of data. Hadoop clusters have to do their work alongside IBM mainframes. Data scientists must somehow get along and work jointly with mere quantitative analysts and database administrators.

In order to understand this coexistence, Jill Dyché of SAS and I interviewed twenty large organizations in the first quarter of 2013 about how big data fit into their overall data and analytics environments. Overall, we found the expected coexistence; in not a single one of these large organizations was big data being managed separately from other types of data and analytics. There were no "Big Data" departments. The integration was in fact leading to a new management perspective on analytics, which I'll call *Analytics 3.0*. In this chapter, I'll describe the overall context for how organizations think about big data, and the organizational structure and skills required for it. I'll conclude by describing the Analytics 3.0 era.

How New?

Big data may be new for start-ups and for online firms, but many large firms view it as something they have been wrestling with for a while. Some managers appreciate the innovative nature of big data but find it business as usual, or part of a continuing evolution toward more data. They have been adding new forms of data to their systems and models for many years and don't see anything revolutionary about big data. Put another way, many were pursuing big data before big data was big.

When these managers in large firms are impressed by big data, it's not the bigness that impresses them. Instead it's one of two other aspects of big data: the lack of structure and the power and low cost of the technologies involved. This is consistent with the results from the survey of more than fifty large companies by NewVantage Partners in

2012 that I mentioned in chapter 1. It found, according to the survey summary:

> *It's about variety, not volume.* The survey indicates companies are focused on the variety of data, not its volume, both today and in three years. The most important goal and potential reward of Big Data initiatives is the ability to analyze diverse data sources and new data types, not managing very large data sets.[1]

Firms that have long handled massive volumes of data are beginning to enthuse about the ability to handle a new type of data—voice or text or log files or images or video. A retail bank, for example, is getting a handle on its multichannel customer interactions for the first time by analyzing log files (it's easier than delving into core transaction systems). A hotel firm is analyzing customer waiting lines with video analytics. A health insurer is able to better predict customer dissatisfaction by analyzing speech-to-text data from call center recordings. In short, these companies can have a much more complete picture of their customers and operations by combining unstructured and structured data.

There are also continuing—if less dramatic—advances from the usage of more structured data from sensors and operational data-gathering devices. Companies like GE, UPS, and Schneider National are increasingly putting sensors into things that move or spin and capturing the resulting data to better optimize their businesses. Even small benefits provide a large payoff when adopted on a large scale. I've mentioned the potential $66 billion savings from more efficient gas turbines, but GE also estimates that a 1 percent fuel reduction from the use of big data from aircraft engines would result in a $30 billion savings for the commercial airline industry over fifteen years.[2] UPS has achieved similarly dramatic savings (see the case study "Big Data at UPS") through better vehicle routing.

Big Data at UPS

UPS is no stranger to big data, having begun to capture and track a variety of package movements and transactions as early as the 1980s. The company now tracks data on 16.3 million packages per day for 8.8 million customers, with an average of 39.5 million tracking requests from customers per day. The company stores over 16 petabytes of data.

Much of its recently acquired big data, however, comes from telematics sensors in over forty-six thousand vehicles. The data on UPS package cars (trucks), for example, includes their speed, direction, braking, and drive-train performance. The data is not only used to monitor daily performance, but to drive a major redesign of UPS drivers' route structures. This initiative, called ORION (on-road integrated optimization and navigation), is arguably the world's largest operations research project. It also relies heavily on online map data and will eventually reconfigure a driver's pickups and drop-offs in real time. The project has already led to savings in 2011 of more than 8.4 million gallons of fuel by cutting 85 million miles off of daily routes. UPS estimates that saving only one daily mile per driver saves the company $30 million, so the overall dollar savings are substantial. The company is also attempting to use data and analytics to optimize the efficiency of its two thousand aircraft flights per day.

Examples of Big Data Objectives in Large Companies

As I noted in chapter 3, big data can bring about dramatic cost reductions, substantial improvements in the time required to perform a computing task, or new product and service offerings. Like traditional analytics, it can also support internal business decisions. The technologies and concepts behind big data allow organizations to achieve a variety of objectives, but most of the large organizations we interviewed were focused on one or two. The chosen objectives have implications for not only the outcome and financial benefits from big data, but also the process—who leads the initiative, where it fits within the organization, and how to manage the project.

Only a few organizations we interviewed were primarily focused on cost reduction. One was the bank, described in chapter 3, that is using Hadoop to take over a variety of computing tasks that had previously been done on other platforms—all for reasons of cost. It's not a bad objective by any means, but I would argue that it should also be combined with other objectives that involve additional revenues or profits.

In chapter 3, I also discussed the second common objective of big data technologies and solutions—time reduction—and described how Macy's and Amadeus are using big data technology to reduce cycle time for reducing merchandise repricing and travel reservation system response time, respectively. One key objective involving time reduction is to be able to interact with the customer in real time, using analytics and data derived from the customer experience. If the customer has "left the building," targeted offers and services are likely to be much less effective. This means rapid data capture, aggregation, processing, and analytics. One company pursuing this type of benefit is Caesars Entertainment. Caesars (formerly Harrah's) has long been a leader in the use of analytics, particularly in the area of customer loyalty, marketing, and service. Today, it is augmenting these traditional analytics capabilities with some big data technologies and skills. The primary objective of exploring and implementing big data tools is to respond in real time for customer marketing and service.

For example, the company has data about its customers from its Total Rewards loyalty program, web clickstreams, and real-time play in slot machines. It has traditionally used all those data sources to understand customers, but it has been difficult to integrate and act on them in real time—that is, while the customer is still playing at a slot machine or in the resort. Caesars has found that if new customers to its loyalty program have a run of bad luck at the slots, it's likely that they will never come back. But if the company can present, say, a free meal coupon to such customers while they're still at the slot machine, they are much more likely to return to the casino later. The key, however, is to do the necessary analysis in real time and present the offer before these customers turn away, disgusted with their luck and the machines at which they've been playing.

In order to pursue this objective and others involving the speed of decision making, Caesars has acquired both Hadoop clusters and open-source and commercial analytics software. It has also added some data scientists to its analytics group.

There are other goals for the big data capabilities as well. Caesars pays fanatical attention—typically through human observation—to ensuring that its most loyal customers don't wait in lines. With video analytics on big data tools, it may be able to employ more automated means for spotting service issues involving less frequent customers. Caesars is also beginning to analyze mobile data and is experimenting with targeted real-time offers to mobile devices.

As with traditional, small-data analytics, big data can also be used to support or improve internal business decisions (see the case study "Big Data at United Healthcare"). These types of decisions employ big data when there are new, less structured data sources that can be applied to the decision. For example, any data that can shed light on customer satisfaction is helpful, and much data from customer interactions is unstructured. I mentioned in chapter 3 that several large banks are using big data to understand multichannel customer relationships—the goal being to identify which customers might be preparing to no longer be customers, or which ones might respond to a particular promotion type.

Big Data at United Healthcare

As I mentioned in chapter 3, United Healthcare is using natural language processing (NLP) to better understand customer satisfaction. It starts by converting records of customer voice calls to its call center into text, and searching for indications that the customer is dissatisfied.

To analyze the text data, United Healthcare uses a variety of tools. The data initially goes into a "data lake" using Hadoop and NoSQL (meaning databases that not only use SQL, the standard for querying and extracting information from relational databases) storage, which require less up-front data manipulation. The NLP—primarily a "singular value decomposition," or modified word count—takes place on a database appliance. A variety of other technologies are being surveyed and tested to assess their fit within the "future state" architecture. United also makes use of interfaces between its statistical analysis tools and Hadoop.

The work to put the customer satisfaction data, along with many other sources of customer data, into a customer data warehouse and analyze it is being led by the finance organization. However, several more of United's functions and units, including its Optum business (specializing in selling data and related services to health-care organizations), are participating. The team includes both conventional quantitative analysts and data scientists with strong IT and data management skills.

United Healthcare, through its subsidiary Optum Labs, is also pursuing a variety of big data analytics projects together with its partner, the Mayo Clinic. It is combining electronic medical records from Mayo and other health-care provider organizations with claims data from United to understand the progression and treatment of disease.

Integrating Organizational Structures and Skills

As with technology architectures, organizational structures and skills for big data in big companies are evolving and integrating with existing structures, rather than being established anew. No organization we interviewed has established an entirely separate organization for big data; instead, existing analytics or technology groups have added big data functions to their missions. Some do not mark any change in organizational structure or skills at all with big data, stating that they have been analyzing large quantities of data for many years. Others simply say that they are adding data science capabilities to their existing portfolios.

The most likely organizational structures to initiate or accommodate big data technologies are either existing analytics groups (including groups with an "operations research" focus, as at UPS and Schneider National); innovation or architectural groups within IT organizations, as at USAA and Procter & Gamble; or R&D analytics groups, as at GE. In many cases these central services organizations are aligned in big data initiatives with analytically oriented functions or business units—marketing, for example, or the online businesses for banks or retailers (see the case study "Big Data at Macys.com"). Some of these business units have IT or analytics groups of their own. The organizations whose approaches seemed most effective and likely to succeed had close relationships between the business groups addressing big data and the IT organizations supporting them.

In terms of skills, most of these large firms are augmenting—or trying to augment—their existing analytical staffs with data scientists who possess a higher level of IT capabilities and the ability to manipulate big data technologies specifically (as compared with traditional quantitative analysts). These might include

Big Data at Macys.com

Macys.com is considered the equivalent of a single store at the giant retailer's structure, but it's growing at a 50 percent annual rate—faster than any other part of the business. The division's management is very oriented to and knowledgeable about IT, data, and analytical decisions. Like other online retailers, Macys.com is heavily focused on customer-oriented analytical applications involving personalization, ad and e-mail targeting, and search engine optimization. Within the Macys.com analytics organization, the "Customer Insights" group addresses these issues, but it also has a "Business Insights" group (focused primarily on supporting and measuring activity around the marketing calendar) and a "Data Science" organization. The latter addresses more leading-edge quantitative techniques involving data mining, marketing, and experimental design.

Macys.com utilizes a variety of leading-edge technologies for big data, most of which are not used elsewhere within the company. They include open-source tools like Hadoop, R, and Impala, as well as purchased software such as SAS, IBM DB2, Vertica, and Tableau. Analytical initiatives are increasingly a blend of traditional data management and analytics technologies and emerging big data tools. The analytics group employs a combination of machine learning approaches and traditional hypothesis-based statistics.

Kerem Tomak, who heads the analytics organization at Macys .com, argues that it's important not to pursue big data technology for its own sake. "We are very ROI-driven, and we only invest in a technology if it solves a business problem for us," he noted. Over time there will be increasing integration between Macys.com and the rest of Macy's systems and data on customers, since Tomak and his colleagues believe that an omnichannel approach to customer relationships is the right direction for the future.

natural language processing or text-mining skills, video or image analytics, and visual analytics. Many of the data scientists are also able to code in scripting languages like Python, Pig, and Hive. In terms of backgrounds, some have PhDs in scientific fields; others are simply strong programmers with some analytical skills. Many of our interviewees questioned whether a data scientist could possess all the needed skills and were taking a team-based approach to assembling them.

A key skill involves explaining big data outcomes to executives, whether in visual displays or verbal narrative. Even among data scientists, several interviewees commented that their quantitative people need to "tell a story with data" and relate well to decision makers. Several representatives in firms we interviewed pointed out that their analytics people are also required to devote considerable time to change management issues. As prescriptive analytical models are embedded into key operational processes, someone needs to work with frontline workers and process owners to bring about needed changes in roles, process designs, and skills.

It goes almost without saying that the skills, processes, and tools necessary to manage exploding amounts of nonstandard data will become ever more important. However, for the most part, the companies we interviewed feel substantially less urgency than the start-ups we have encountered with regard to data science talent. For some, however, the talent shortage is beginning to bite.

The most active recruiter of data scientists among the large companies we interviewed is GE, which has an objective of recruiting roughly four hundred of them and has already hired or transferred in from elsewhere in GE about half that many. Although GE has had considerable success in recruiting data scientists, it is also creating an internally developed training program. It also occasionally has challenges recruiting data scientists who are familiar with the specific data issues around its industrial products (e.g., turbine sensor data).

Several companies also mentioned the need for combining data scientist skills with traditional data management virtues. Solid knowledge of data architectures, metadata, data quality and correction processes, data stewardship and administration dashboards, master data management hubs, matching algorithms, and a host of other data-specific topics are important for firms pursuing big data as a long-term strategic differentiator.

Whatever the organizational structure for managing big data in large firms, data-savvy leadership is also necessary. In 2011 a widely read McKinsey report on big data cited a company's "data-driven mind-set" to be a key indicator of big data's value to companies.[3] The report gauged corporate cultures of fact-based decision making (as opposed to gut feel) as an important indicator of big data's value potential. The report also argued that in the United States alone, more than 1.5 million data-savvy managers would be needed to lead their organizations' big data initiatives.

But effective managers in leading firms have already deduced how big data will drive value for their companies, using stories of big data successes to justify their own efforts. Likewise they use stories of missteps and false starts to establish solid business cases and firm up their planning and deployment strategies. As the McKinsey study noted, "Many pioneering companies are already using big data to create value, and others need to explore how they can do the same if they are to compete."

The executives we interviewed are part of the latter group who have convinced their leadership and constituents that launching big data is not only worthwhile, but worth more than it costs. Many have responsibilities not only for big data and analytics, but for other functions as well (see the case study "Big Data at Bank of America").

Big Data at Bank of America

Given Bank of America's large size in assets (over $2.2 trillion in 2012) and customer base (52 million consumers and small businesses), it was arguably in the big data business many years ago. Today the bank is focusing on big data, but with an emphasis on an integrated approach to customers and an integrated organizational structure. It thinks of big data in three different buckets—big transactional data, data about customers, and unstructured data. The primary emphasis is on the first two categories.

With a very large amount of customer data across multiple channels and relationships, the bank historically was unable to analyze all of its customers at once, relying instead on systematic samples. With big data technology, it can increasingly process and analyze data from its full customer set.

Other than some experiments with analysis of unstructured data, the primary focus of the bank's big data efforts is on understanding the customer across all channels and interactions, and presenting consistent, appealing offers to well-defined customer segments. A new program of "BankAmeriDeals" provides cash-back offers to holders of the bank's credit and debit cards based on analyses of where they have made payments in the past. There is also an effort to understand the nature of and satisfaction from customer journeys across a variety of distribution channels, including online, call center, and retail branch interactions.

The bank has historically employed a large number of quantitative analysts, but for the big data era they have been consolidated and restructured, with matrixed reporting lines to both a central analytics group and to business functions and units. The consumer banking analytics group, for example, made up of the quantitative analysts and data scientists, reports to Aditya Bhasin, who also heads Consumer Marketing and Digital Banking. It is working more closely with business line executives than ever before.

Big Data's Value Proposition

When I talked to big-company executives about big data for this chapter, they all agreed that they considered big data to be an evolutionary set of capabilities that would have new and sometimes unanticipated uses over time. But every one of these executives conceded that they couldn't afford to make big data a mere academic exercise. It needed to drive value, and better sooner than later. For some, like Citigroup, big data technologies had to pay their way through rapid cost reduction (see the case study "Big Data at Citigroup"). These firms had little use for big data simply as a shiny new management object.

Big Data at Citigroup

Citigroup has been a data-driven financial services firm since before many of its competitors were in business. Founded in 1812 as City Bank of New York, the financial services conglomerate has evolved to serve 200 million consumer and institutional customers across 160 countries. The wider the company's reach, the greater the role of big data in its strategy.

The subject of corporate information—its integration, its quality, and its growing volumes—was a natural by-product of executive-level conversations around regulatory and competitive demands. In 2010, the company established a Chief Data Office. Shortly thereafter, the company downloaded Hadoop and began reengineering computation-heavy data transformations using the big data environment. A major focus of the Hadoop implementation is cost reduction.

The firm's plans include expanding that environment to refine its understanding of customer relationships and behaviors. On the consumer side, Citi is establishing relationships between so-called "white label" cards and commercial cards to detect potential increases in credit risk. And on the business side, the firm can view high-value transaction data and create custom supply chains or fine-tune financing structures for counterparties in commercial transactions. The low-cost, high-performance nature of its Hadoop infrastructure also gives Citi the ability to dynamically deploy targeted digital offers to customers' mobile devices when they step over a "geographic gate."

Return on Investment

Among big data start-ups and online businesses, the success of the big data initiative is basically the success of the business model—so few bother to analyze the returns from big data alone. And very few large companies have taken the steps to rigorously quantify the return on investment for their big data efforts. The reality is that the proof points about big data often transcend hard dollars represented by cost savings or revenue generation. This suggests that senior management is betting on big data for the long term, a point corroborated by several of the executives we interviewed.

But initial comparisons of big data ROI are more than promising; I presented some cost-reduction figures from one company in chapter 3. For another source, in 2011, Wikibon, an open-source knowledge sharing community, published a case study that compared the financial return of two analytics environments.[4] The first was a high-speed data warehouse appliance employing traditional extract, transform, and load (ETL) approaches and data provisioning processes. The second environment was big data running on a newer big data technology using massively parallel processing (MPP) hardware and Hadoop.

As figure 8-1 shows, the project favored the MPP/Hadoop big data environment across a range of measures, including accelerating time-to-value (it showed value almost immediately after installation), cumulative cash flow, and internal rate of return. (The findings became part of a larger discussion in the Wikibon community, which asked the question, "Is your data warehouse a dinosaur?") The study's conclusion was not that the data warehouse was becoming obsolete, but rather that traditional data warehouses would end up peacefully coexisting with emerging big data solutions, each playing a specialized role in a company's analytics ecosystem.

The truth is that executives at big data early-adopter companies don't talk about how much money they're saving or making. Those we interviewed described two approaches for realizing return on big data. One approach was enabling new business capabilities for the first time. The other was doing what they were already doing with data and analytics—usually making decisions—only cheaper, faster, or better than before. Although few of these firms are undertaking serious cost or benefit measurement for big data projects, the latter benefit would be easier to measure.

Automating Existing Processes

Whether they need to do a proof-of-concept, explore preliminary data, or convince executives to invest, many companies have to prove the value of big data technologies as a first step to broader big data

FIGURE 8-1

ROI comparison for big data

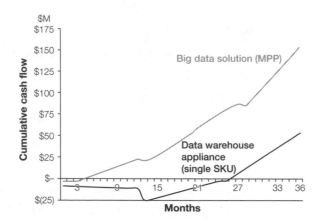

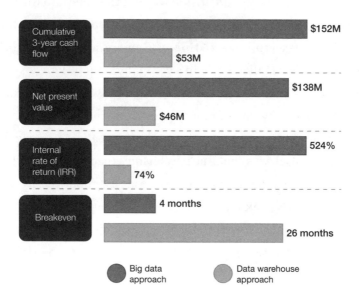

Source: http://wikibon.org/wiki/v/Financial_Comparison_of_Big_Data_MPP_Solution_and_Data_Warehouse_Appliance.

delivery. This often means delivering cost efficiencies or economies of scale within existing business paradigms.

Most of the executives we interviewed introduced big data technologies through an initial proof-of-concept approach to illustrate the high performance, lower cost of ownership, scale, and advanced business capabilities of big data solutions by applying them to current, often cumbersome, business processes. In some cases the proofs of concept showed the need for changes in other processes. At a major US airline, for example, analysis of call center speech-to-text data showed that customer interactions with call centers could be useful in predicting customer behavior, but also that call center processes needed some basic improvements that were more important than finer-grained predictive models.

Other companies see the promise of big data to bring together disparate platform and processing functions that were previously fragmented and siloed. The executives I interviewed spoke aspirationally of the ability to combine data reporting, analytics, exploration, protection, and recovery functions on a single big data platform, thereby eliminating the need for complicated programming and specialized skills to tie legacy systems together. They don't expect this to happen anytime soon, however. Some, like Sears Holdings (see the case study "Big Data at Sears Holdings"), are making major investments in supplying "data as a service" to make big data analysis a pervasive phenomenon throughout their organizations.

The good news about applying new technology to existing problems is that opportunities for improvement are already well understood, and thus consensus is more easily achieved. One banking vice president explained, "Fixing what's known to be slow or broken gets more support from my CEO than promoting new technologies out of the box. He doesn't care whether our competitors are using big data. He cares that they could be gaining market share by making faster decisions."

Big Data at Sears Holdings

When it comes to the adoption of information technology, Sears was years ahead of most retailers, implementing an enterprise data warehouse in the 1980s while most retailers were still relying on manually updated spreadsheets to examine their sales numbers. These days, the company is using big data technologies to accelerate the integration of petabytes of customer, product, sales, and campaign data in order to understand how to increase marketing returns and bring customers back into its stores. The retailer uses Hadoop to not only store but also process data transformations and integrate heterogeneous data more quickly and efficiently than ever.

"We're investing in real-time data acquisition as it happens," says Oliver Ratzesberger, (at the time of the interview) Vice President of Information Analytics and Innovation at Sears Holdings. "No more ETL. Big data technologies make it easy to eliminate sources of latency that have built up over a period of time." The company is now leveraging open-source projects Apache Kafka and Storm to enable real-time processing. "Our goal is to be able to measure what's just happened."

The company's CTO, Phil Shelley (who has since left to start his own big data company), has cited big data's capability to decrease the release of a set of complex marketing campaigns from eight weeks to one week—and the improvements are still being realized. Faster and more targeted campaigns are just the tip of the iceberg for the retailer, which recently launched a subsidiary, MetaScale, to provide non-retailers with big data services in the cloud.

"Sears is investing in real-time data acquisition and integration as it happens," says Ratzesberger. "We're bringing in open-source solutions and changing our applications architecture. We're creating a framework that, over time, any application can leverage."

Moreover, it's easier to measure new process improvements against traditional methods, so quantifying faster product time to market, higher return on marketing investment, or fewer patient readmissions makes quantifying return on investment that much easier.

Delivering the New

But even executives advocating large-scale change have their eye on the shiny, new capabilities promised by big data analytics. One of most aspects of big data is the way it has captured the attention of senior managers like no other technology trend before it. Suddenly, C-level executives are funding headcount for big data projects and using the phrase "data as an asset" in board meetings.

New applications for big data are often industry-specific. Think telematics data for auto insurers, vital signs in health care, or RFID tags in manufacturing. All of this data is difficult to capture and ingest, let alone use in a meaningful way. A recent survey found that the highest percentage of respondents—41 percent—reported not having a strategy for big data. The next-largest group reported "Operations/Processing" as being the area of focus for big data projects.[5]

Clearly, most companies still haven't transcended their initial projects to articulate the full business potential of big data. It's still early days. And fundamental questions persist: Is big data best consumed by humans or machines? Is our most important data about our customers or our operations? Will new data drive new insights or simply confirm existing hypotheses? Most big companies are launching their big data projects starting with automation of existing processes and hoping to drive more strategic value. In most cases, that value is in the eye of the beholder.

The Rise of Analytics 3.0

In order to understand the role of big data in big companies, it's important to understand the historical context for analytics and the brief history of big data. The three eras of analytical orientation are described in table 8-1.

Analytics, of course, are not a new idea. The tools have been used in business since the mid-1950s. To be sure, there has been a recent explosion of interest in the topic, but for the first half-century of activity, the way analytics were pursued in most organizations didn't change that much. We'll call the initial era *Analytics 1.0*. This period, which stretched fifty-five years—from 1954 (when UPS initiated the first corporate analytics group in the United States) to about 2005—was characterized by the following attributes:

- Data sources were relatively small and structured, and came from internal sources.

- Data had to be stored in enterprise warehouses or marts before analysis.

TABLE 8-1

Three eras of analytics

	Analytics 1.0	Analytics 2.0	Analytics 3.0
Types of companies	Large enterprises	Online and start-ups	All—"data economy"
Analytics objective	Internal decisions	New products	Decisions and products
Data type	Small, structured	Large, unstructured	All types combined
Creation approach	Long-cycle batch	Short-cycle agile	Short-cycle agile
Primary technology	Software packages	Open source	Broad portfolio
Primary analytics type	Descriptive	Descriptive, predictive	Prescriptive
Business relationship	Back office	"On the bridge"	Collaborative

- The great majority of analytical activity was descriptive analytics, or reporting.

- Creating analytical models was a "batch" process often requiring several months.

- Quantitative analysts were segregated from business people and decisions in back offices.

- Very few organizations competed on analytics—for most, analytics were marginal to their strategy.

Data science first began to be discussed in earnest by academics around 2001; the Purdue statistician William S. Cleveland published a paper advocating for the field in that year, and in the following two years two new journals of data science were created.[6] Beginning in 2003 or so, the commercial world began to take notice of big data, and let's call the early 2000s the beginning of *Analytics 2.0*. The era began with the exploitation of online data in internet-based firms like Google, Yahoo!, and eBay—the earliest adopters of the "data economy." Big data and analytics not only informed internal decisions, but also formed the basis for customer-facing products and processes. However, at this time, large companies often confined their analytical efforts to internal information domains like customer or product that were highly structured and rarely integrated with other data. In other words, they stuck with Analytics 1.0 for the most part.

Big data analytics as a stand-alone entity in Analytics 2.0 were quite different from the 1.0 era in many ways. Data was often externally sourced and, as the term *big data* suggests, was either very large or unstructured. The fast flow of data meant that it had to be stored and processed rapidly, often with massively parallel servers running Hadoop. The overall speed of analysis was much faster. Visual analytics—a form

Big Data at Verizon Wireless

Verizon Wireless, a joint venture of Verizon Communications and Vodaphone Group, is no different from other wireless carriers in having a great deal of information about its customer movements. All wireless phones broadcast their location (accurate within thirty feet) in radio signals, and all carriers capture the information. Now, however, in a business unit called Precision Market Insights, Verizon is selling information about how often mobile phone users are in certain locations and their activities and backgrounds. Customers thus far have included malls, stadium owners, and billboard firms.

For the Phoenix Suns, an NBA basketball team, Precision Market Insights offered the following information:

- Where people attending the team's games live (and hence where people who don't attend games live) in order to target team advertising

- How many game attendees are from out of town (about 22 percent in one month studied)

- The attributes of attendees (most likely between twenty-five to fifty-four years old, with household incomes of more than $50,000, and parents with children at home)

- How often attendees also attend baseball spring training games in the Phoenix area (13 percent)

- Increases in traffic at a fast-food chain within twenty-four hours of a game that are linked to a Suns promotion (8.4 percent)

The value of this information to customers is perhaps obvious; a Phoenix Suns executive commented, "This is the information that everyone has wanted that hasn't been available until now."

Source: Information in this Verizon case study comes from a company interview, the Verizon Precision Market Insights website, and Anton Troianovski, "Phone Firms Sell Data on Customers," *Wall Street Journal*, May 22, 2013.

of descriptive analytics—often crowded out predictive and prescriptive analytical techniques. The new generation of quantitative analysts was called *data scientists*, and many were not content with working in the back room; they wanted to work on new product offerings and to help shape the business; they wanted to be "on the bridge."

Big data, of course, is still a popular concept, and one might think that we're still in the 2.0 period. However, there is considerable evidence from our research that large organizations are entering the *Analytics 3.0* era—one that's qualitatively different from either 1.0 or 2.0. It's an environment that combines the best of 1.0 and 2.0—a blend of big data and traditional analytics that yields insights and offerings with speed and impact. Although it's early days for this new model, the traits of Analytics 3.0 are already becoming apparent. The most important is that not only online firms, but virtually any type of firm in any industry, can participate in the data-driven economy. Banks, industrial manufacturers, health-care providers, retailers, telecom firms (see the case study "Big Data at Verizon Wireless")—any company in any industry that is willing to exploit the possibilities—can all develop data-based offerings for customers, as well as supporting internal decisions with big data.

Other attributes of Analytics 3.0 organizations are described next.

Multiple Data Types, Often Combined

Organizations are combining large and small volumes of data, internal and external sources, and structured and unstructured formats to yield new insights in predictive and prescriptive models. Often the increased number of data sources is incremental, rather than a revolutionary advance in capability. For example, at trucking

Big Data at Schneider National

Schneider National, one of North America's largest trucking, logistics, and intermodal services providers, has been pursuing various forms of analytical optimization for a couple of decades. What has changed in Schneider's business over the past several years is the availability of low-cost sensors for its trucks, trailers, and intermodal containers. The sensors monitor location, driving behaviors, fuel levels, and whether a trailer/container is loaded or empty. Schneider has been transitioning to a new technology platform over the last five years, but leaders there don't draw a bright line between big data and more traditional data types. However, the quality of the optimized decisions it makes with the sensor data—dispatching of trucks and containers, for example—is improving substantially, and the company's use of prescriptive analytics is changing job roles and relationships.

New sensors are constantly becoming available. For example, fuel-level sensors, which Schneider is beginning to implement, allow better fueling optimization (identifying the optimal location at which a driver should stop for fuel based on how much is left in the tank, the truck's destination, and fuel prices along the way). In the past, drivers have entered the data manually, but sensor data is both more accurate and free of bias.

Safety is a core value at Schneider. Driving sensors pick up data, tracked in dashboard-based safety metrics that relate to driving risks. Hard braking in a truck, for example, is captured by sensors and relayed to headquarters, triggering discussions between drivers and their leaders. Schneider is piloting a process in which the sensor data, along with other factors, goes into a model that predicts which drivers may be at greater risk of a safety incident. The use of predictive analytics produces a score that initiates a preemptive conversation with the driver and leads to fewer safety-related incidents.

firm Schneider National, the company is increasingly adding data from new sensors to its logistical optimization algorithms. These sensors monitor key indicators to substantially improve business processes and reduce costs (see the case study "Big Data at Schneider National").

Much Faster Technologies and Methods

Big data technologies include a variety of hardware/software architectures, including clustered parallel servers using Hadoop/MapReduce, dedicated big data appliances, in-memory analytics, in-database processing, and so forth. All of these technologies are considerably faster than previous generations of technology for data management and analysis. Analyses that might have taken hours or days in the past can be done in seconds. To complement the faster technologies, new agile (or even faster) analytical methods and machine learning techniques are being employed that produce insights at a much faster rate. Like agile system development, these methods involve frequent delivery of partial outputs to project stakeholders; as with the best data scientists' work, there is an ongoing sense of urgency. The challenge is adapting operational and decision processes to take advantage of what the new technologies and methods can bring forth.

Integrated and Embedded Models

Consistent with the increased speed of analytics and data processing, analytical models in Analytics 3.0 are often being embedded into operational and decision processes, dramatically increasing their speed and impact. I discussed this phenomenon in chapter 6 with regard to Heathrow Airport, but it is happening at a variety of other companies as well. At Procter & Gamble, for example, a set of "business sufficiency models"—defined as all the information needed to manage the business in seven key domains—are included in two major decision environments. One, called the Decision Cockpit, is present on over fifty thousand desktops at P&G. Another environment, called the Business Sphere, is used for management decision making in groups, and features a room in which large screens show visual analytics displays. Business Spheres are present in more than fifty P&G facilities around the world. In other organizations, models are embedded into fully automated systems based on scoring algorithms or analytics-based rules. Some are built into consumer-oriented products and features. In any case, embedding the analytics into systems and processes not only means greater speed, but also makes it more difficult for decision makers to avoid using analytics—usually a good thing.

New and Hybrid Technology Environments

It's clear that the Analytics 3.0 environment involves new technology architectures, but it's a hybrid of well-understood and emerging tools. The existing technology environment for large organizations is not being disbanded; some of the firms I researched still make effective use of relational databases on IBM mainframes. However, there is a greater use of big data technologies like Hadoop on commodity server clusters, cloud technologies (private and public), and open-source software. The most notable changes are attempts to eliminate the tedious ETL step before data can be assessed and analyzed. This objective is being addressed through real-time messaging and computation tools such as Apache Kafka and Storm.

A related approach being explored is a new discovery platform layer of technology for data exploration. Enterprise data warehouses were initially intended for exploration and analysis, but they have become production data repositories for many organizations, and getting data into them requires expensive and time-consuming ETL work. Hence the need for a new layer that facilitates data discovery.

The result of these changes is that the complexity and number of choices that IT architects have to make about data management have expanded considerably, and almost every organization will end up with a hybrid environment. The old formats haven't gone away, but new processes need to be developed by which data and the focal point for analysis will move across staging, evaluation, exploration, and production applications.

Data Science/Analytics/IT Teams

Data scientists often are able to run the whole show—or at least have a lot of independence—in online firms and big data start-ups. In more conventional large firms, however, they have to collaborate with a variety of other players. In many cases the "data scientists" in large firms may be conventional quantitative analysts who are forced to spend a bit more time than they like on data management activities (which is hardly a new phenomenon). And the data hackers who excel at extracting and structuring data are working with conventional quantitative analysts who excel at modeling it. Both groups have to work with IT, who supply the big data and analytical infrastructure and provision the sandboxes, or data discovery environments, in which these groups can explore data and turn exploratory analyses into production capabilities. Together the combined teams are doing whatever is necessary to get the analytical job done, and there is often a lot of overlap across roles.

Chief Analytics Officers (or Equivalent)

It wouldn't make sense for companies to have multiple leaders for different types of data, so they are beginning to create *chief analytics officer* roles or equivalent titles to oversee the building of analytical capabilities. As I mentioned in chapter 6, AIG brought in long-term analytics leader Murli Buluswar to be chief science officer. His staff works on traditional insurance problems (e.g., analytical pricing optimization) and is collaborating with MIT researchers on big data projects. Buluswar is representative of this new type of leader under Analytics 3.0. Other organizations, including FICO, the University of Pittsburgh Medical Center, the Obama re-election campaign, and the insurer USAA, have identified chief analytics officers as well.

Increased Use of Prescriptive Analytics

There have always been three types of analytics: descriptive, which report on the past; predictive, which use models based on past data to predict the future; and prescriptive, which use models to specify optimal behaviors and actions. Analytics 3.0 includes all types, but there is an increased emphasis on prescriptive analytics. These models involve large-scale testing and optimization. They are a means of embedding analytics into key processes and employee behaviors. They provide a high level of operational benefits for organizations, but they place a premium on high-quality planning and execution.

Prescriptive analytics also can change the roles of frontline employees and their relationships with supervisors, as at Schneider National and UPS. If computers and analytics are telling you how to drive, where to go next, where to stop, or that you have stopped too hard or made an inappropriate left turn against traffic, it leads to an entirely new way of thinking about your job. The data and analytics had better be right, or it will be difficult to ever recover trust.

Summary

Even though it's been only a decade since the advent of big data (or at least the awareness of it), its attributes add up to a new era. It is clear from my research that large organizations across industries are joining the data economy and using big data not only for better and faster decisions and lower costs, but also for new data-based products and services for customers. They are not keeping traditional analytics and big data separate, but are combining them to form a new synthesis. Some aspects of Analytics 3.0 and the use of data and analytics in large firms will no doubt continue to emerge, but organizations need to begin transitioning now to the new model. It means change in skills, leadership, organizational structures, technologies, and architectures. It is perhaps the most sweeping change in what we do to get value from data since the 1980s.

As I noted in chapter 1, the primary value from big data comes not from the data in its raw form (no matter how big it is), but from the processing and analysis of it and the insights, products, and services that emerge from analysis. The sweeping changes in big data technologies and management approaches need to be accompanied by similarly dramatic shifts in how data supports decisions and product/service innovation. There is little doubt that analytics can transform organizations, and the firms that lead the 3.0 charge will seize the most value.

Big Data in Big Companies—Analytics 3.0

- Do you have innovative products and services based on data and analytics?

- Are you adding large volumes of unstructured data to the mix of data that your organization analyzes and benefits from?

- Are you embedding analytics into your most important operational and decision processes?

- Are you beginning to use analytics to tell managers and workers how to perform better in their jobs?

- Are you integrating new big data technologies into the data warehouses and analytical technology architectures at your firm?

- Have you attracted new employees with a mixture of analytical and computer science skills?

- Have you elevated your head of analytics and big data to be a senior executive within the organization?

Appendix

Big Data Readiness Assessment Survey

This assessment survey can be used to determine your organization's readiness for big data projects. It follows the DELTTA model described in chapter 6. There are five questions for each of the DELTTA factors. Each can be answered with a Likert scale response similar to the following:

1. Disagree strongly

2. Disagree somewhat

3. Neither agree nor disagree

4. Agree somewhat

5. Agree strongly

Unless there is some reason to weight some questions or areas more than others, I would recommend averaging the scores within each DELTTA factor to create an overall score. It may also be useful to combine the factor scores to create an overall readiness score.

The following questions are largely modified from a set used by the International Institute for Analytics to assess analytical capabilities. I have also drawn in small measure from questions created to assess big data readiness by MIT researchers Erik Brynjolfsson and Andy McAfee.[1]

The questions can be applied to an entire organization or to a business unit within it. Whoever replies to the questions should be familiar with the entire organization or unit's approaches to big data.

Data

_____   We have access to very large, unstructured, or fast-moving data for analysis.

_____   We integrate data from multiple internal sources into a data warehouse or mart for easy access.

_____   We integrate external data with internal to facilitate high-value analysis of our business environment.

_____   We maintain consistent definitions and standards across the data we use for analysis.

_____   Users, decision makers, and product developers trust the quality of our data.

Enterprise

_____   We employ a combination of big data and traditional analytics approaches to achieve our organization's goals.

_____ Our organization's management ensures that business units and functions collaborate to determine big data and analytics priorities for the organization.

_____ We structure our data scientists and analytical professionals to enable learning and capabilities sharing across the organization.

_____ Our big data and analytics initiatives and infrastructure receive adequate funding and other resources to build the capabilities we need.

_____ We collaborate with channel partners, customers, and other members of our business ecosystem to share big data content and applications.

Leadership

_____ Our senior executives regularly consider the opportunities that big data and analytics might bring to our business.

_____ Our senior executives challenge business unit and functional leaders to incorporate big data and analytics into their decision-making and business processes.

_____ Senior executives in our organization utilize big data and analytics to guide both strategic and tactical decisions.

_____ Non-executive level managers in our organization utilize big data and analytics to guide their decisions.

_____ Our process for prioritizing and deploying our big data assets (data, people, software and hardware) is directed and reviewed by senior management.

Targets

_____ We prioritize our big data efforts to high-value opportunities to differentiate us from our competitors.

_____ We consider new products and services based on big data as an aspect of our innovation process.

_____ We identify internal opportunities for big data and analytics by evaluating our processes, strategies, and marketplace.

_____ We regularly conduct data-driven experiments to gather data on what works and what doesn't in our business.

_____ We evaluate our existing decisions supported by analytics and data to assess whether new, unstructured data sources could provide better models.

Technology

_____ We have explored or adopted parallel computing approaches (e.g., Hadoop) to big data processing.

_____ We are adept at using data visualization to illuminate a business issue or decision.

_____ We have explored or adopted cloud-based services for processing data and doing analytics.

_____ We have explored or adopted open-source software for big data and analytics.

_____ We have explored or adopted tools to process unstructured data such as text, video, or images.

Analysts and Data Scientists

_____   We have a sufficient number of capable data scientists and analytics professionals to achieve our analytical objectives.

_____   Our data scientists and analytics professionals act as trusted consultants to our senior executives on key decisions and data-driven innovation.

_____   Our data scientists and analytical professionals understand the business disciplines and processes to which big data and analytics are being applied.

_____   Our data scientists, quantitative analysts, and data management professionals operate effectively in teams to address big data and analytics projects.

_____   We have programs (either internal or in partnership with external organizations) to develop data science and analytical skills in our employees.

Notes

Chapter 1

1. John Gantz and David Reinsel, *Big Data, Bigger Digital Shadows, and Biggest Growth in the Far East*, International Data Corporation Digital Universe study, December 1, 2012, http://www.emc.com/collateral/analyst-reports/idc-the-digital-universe-in-2020.pdf.

2. Study on data scientists: Thomas H. Davenport, *The Human Side of Big Data and High-Performance Analytics* (sponsored by SAS and EMC), http://www.sas.com/reg/gen/corp/2154478; study on big data in big companies: Thomas H. Davenport and Jill Dyché, *Big Data in Big Companies Research Report* (sponsored by SAS), www.sas.com/reg/gen/corp/2266746; study of big data in the travel industry: Thomas H. Davenport, *At the Big Data Crossroads: Turning Toward a Smarter Travel Experience* (sponsored by Amadeus), www.amadeus.com/bigdata; study of data discovery: sponsored by Teradata Aster (not yet completed at the time of this book's publication).

3. NewVantage Partners, *Big Data Executive Survey: Themes and Trends*, 2012, http://newvantage.com/data-management/. I am an adviser to NewVantage Partners.

4. Dan Power's *A Brief History of Decision Support Systems* has more detail on some of the early terminology; see http://dssresources.com/history/dsshistory.html.

5. The 2.5-quintillion-byte estimate comes from IBM, "What Is Big Data? Bringing Big Data to the Enterprise," www.ibm.com.

6. H. James Wilson, "You, by the Numbers," *Harvard Business Review*, September 2012, 119–122.

7. Stephen Wolfram, "The Personal Analytics of My Life," blog post, March 8, 2012, http://blog.stephenwolfram.com/2012/03/the-personal-analytics-of-my-life/.

8. http://www.unglobalpulse.org/technology/hunchworks.

9. Steve Lohr, "Searching Big Data for Digital Smoke Signals," *New York Times*, August 7, 2013, http://www.nytimes.com/2013/08/08/technology/development-groups-tap-big-data-to-direct-humanitarian-aid.html.

10. I am grateful to Paul Barth for many of the ideas in this section on experimentation. Some of them appeared in Thomas H. Davenport, Paul Barth, and Randy Bean, "How Big Data Is Different," *MIT Sloan Management Review* (Fall 2012), http://sloanreview.mit.edu/the-magazine/2012-fall/54104/how-big-data-is-different/.

11. Schwartz was interviewed by Paul Barth and Randy Bean for "How Big Data Is Different."

12. Spencer Ackerman, "Welcome to the Age of Big Drone Data," *Wired.com*, April 25, 2013, http://www.wired.com/dangerroom/2013/04/drone-sensors-big-data/.

13. Michael Hayden, "Ex-CIA Chief: What Edward Snowden Did," *CNN.com*, July 19, 2013, http://www.cnn.com/2013/07/19/opinion/hayden-snowden-impact.

14. Peter Drucker, "The Next Information Revolution," *Forbes ASAP*, August 24, 1998.

15. Thomas H. Davenport, "Recorded Future: Analyzing Internet Ideas About What Comes Next," Case 613-083 (Boston: Harvard Business School, 2013).

16. Anand Rajaram, "More Data Usually Beats Better Algorithms," *Datawocky* (blog), http://anand.typepad.com/datawocky/2008/03/more-data-usual.html.

17. Alon Halevy, Peter Norvig, and Fernando Pereira, "The Unreasonable Effectiveness of Data," *IEEE Intelligent Systems,* March 2009, 8–12.

18. Pew Research Center, *Internet Users Don't Like Targeted Ads*, March 13, 2012, http://www.pewresearch.org/daily-number/internet-users-dont-like-targeted-ads/.

19. Andrew McAfee and Erik Brynjolfsson, "Big Data: The Management Revolution," *Harvard Business Review*, October 2012, 60–68.

Chapter 2

1. "88 Acres: How Microsoft Quietly Built the City of the Future," http://www.microsoft.com/en-us/news/stories/88acres/88-acres-how-microsoft-quietly-built-the-city-of-the-future-chapter-1.aspx.

2. Stephanie Clifford and Quentin Hardy, "Attention, Shoppers: Store Is Tracking Your Cell," *New York Times*, June 14, 2013, http://www.nytimes.com/2013/07/15/business/attention-shopper-stores-are-tracking-your-cell.html.

3. Emily Singer, "The Measured Life," *Technology Review*, June 21, 2011, http://www.technologyreview.com/featuredstory/424390/the-measured-life/.

4. IBM Corporation, "Mobile Isn't a Device, It's Data," www.ibm.com/mobilefirst/us/en/bin/pdf/wsj0429opad.pdf.

5. Neustar, "Solution Sheet" for AccountLink service, http://www.neustar.biz/information/docs/pdfs/solutionsheets/accountlink-solutionsheet.pdf.

6. David Carr, "Giving Viewers What They Want," *New York Times*, February 24, 2013, http://www.nytimes.com/2013/02/25/business/media/for-house-of-cards-using-big-data-to-guarantee-its-popularity.html.

7. GTM Research, *The Soft Grid 2013–2020*, study sponsored by SAS Institute, 2013, http://www.sas.com/news/analysts/Soft_Grid_2013_2020_Big_Data_Utility_Analytics_Smart_Grid.pdf.

8. Wes Nichols, "Advertising Analytics 2.0," *Harvard Business Review*, March 2013, 60–68.

9. John Brockman interview with Alex (Sandy) Pentland, "Reinventing Society in the Wake of Big Data," *Edge*, August 30, 2012, http://www.edge.org/conversation/reinventing-society-in-the-wake-of-big-data.

10. Full disclosure: I am an adviser to Signals Intelligence Group.

Chapter 3

1. Clint Boulton, "GameStop CIO: Hadoop Isn't for Everyone," *Wall Street Journal* CIO Journal site, December 10, 2012, http://blogs.wsj.com/cio/2012/12/10/gamestop-cio-hadoop-isnt-for-everyone/.

2. The interview of this manager, who wished to remain unnamed, was conducted by the author and Jill Dyché by telephone on February 17, 2013.

3. GroupM's use of big data is described in Joel Schectman, "Ad Firm Finds Way to Cut Big Data Costs," *Wall Street Journal* CIO Journal website, February 8, 2013, http://blogs.wsj.com/cio/2013/02/08/ad-firm-finds-way-to-cut-big-data-costs/.

4. Kerem Tomak, in "Two Expert Perspectives on High-Performance Analytics," *Intelligence Quarterly* (a SAS publication), 2nd quarter (2012): 6.

5. The interview of this manager, who wished to remain anonymous, was conducted by the author by telephone on March 19, 2013.

6. Tom Vanderbilt, "Let the Robot Drive: The Autonomous Car of the Future Is Here," *Wired*, January 20, 2012, http://www.wired.com/magazine/2012/01/ff_autonomouscars/.

7. Joe Jimenez interview with Geoffrey Colvin, "Joe Jimenez Lays Out His Path to Business Longevity," *Fortune*, March 21, 2013, http://money.cnn.com/2013/03/21/news/companies/novartis-joe-jimenez.pr.fortune/index.html.

8. In-person and e-mail discussions between author and Joey Fitts of Matters Corp., September 2013. I subsequently became an adviser to Fitts' company.

9. Thomas C. Redman, "Building Data Discovery Into Your Organization," *Harvard Business Review* blog post, http://blogs.hbr.org/cs/2012/05/building_data_discovery_into_y.html.

10. Amadeus interviews (some in-person, some by telephone) were conducted in January and February 2013 for "Big Data in the Travel Industry," a research project sponsored by the company; see Thomas H. Davenport, *At the Big Data Crossroads: Turning Toward a Smarter Travel Experience*, June 2013, www.amadeus.com/bigdata.

11. In-person and telephone interviews with Lisa Hook, April 2013 and June 2013, respectively.

Chapter 4

1. In-person discussion with Blaise Heltai and further discussion by e-mail, March 2013.

2. Jake Porway, "You Can't Just Hack Your Way to Social Change," *Harvard Business Review* blog post, March 7, 2013, http://blogs.hbr.org/cs/2013/03/you_cant_just_hack_your_way_to.html.

3. Bill Goodwin, "Poor Communication to Blame for Business Intelligence Failure, Says Gartner," *ComputerWeekly.com*, January 10, 2011, http://www.computerweekly.com/news/1280094776/Poor-communication-toblame for business-intelligence-failure-says-Gartner.

4. See Thomas H. Davenport and Jinho Kim, *Keeping Up with the Quants* (Boston: Harvard Business Review Press, 2013).

5. Sinan Aral with visualization by Nikolaos Hanselmann, "To Go from Big Data to Big Insight, Start with a Visual," August 27, 2013, *Harvard Business Review* blog post, http://blogs.hbr.org/2013/08/visualizing-how-online-word-of/.

6. Vincent Granville, "Vertical vs. Horizontal Data Scientists," *Data Science Central* blog post, March 17, 2013, http://www.datasciencecentral.com/profiles/blogs/vertical-vs-horizontal-data-scientists.

7. Panel discussion at conference and e-mail correspondence with Mark Grabb, March–April 2013.

8. Talent Analytics, "Benchmarking Analytical Talent," 2012, http://www.talentanalytics.com/talent-analytics-corp/research-study/.

9. E-mail correspondence with Mark Grabb, April 1, 2013.

10. Barbara Wixom et al., "The Current State of Business Intelligence in Academia," *Communications of the Association for Information Systems* 29 (2011), http://aisel.aisnet.org/cais/vol29/iss1/16.

11. Interview with Jake Klamka conducted by DJ Patil, my coauthor on the article "Data Scientist: The Sexiest Job of the 21st Century," *Harvard Business Review*, October 2012, 70–76.

12. Thanks to DJ Patil for telling me about Greylock's work with data scientists. He was then the Chief Data Scientist in Residence at Greylock.

13. Telephone interview with Amy Heineike, February 28, 2012.

14. Sy Mukherjee, "Could IBM's 'Watson' Supercomputer Be the Future of U.S. Healthcare Information Technology?" *ThinkProgress*, February 26, 2013, http://thinkprogress.org/health/2013/02/26/1637641/ibm-watson-supercomputer/.

15. See, for example, James Taylor, *Decision Management Systems: A Practical Guide to Using Business Rules and Predictive Analytics* (Indianapolis, IN: IBM Press, 2011), or Taylor's website, www.jtonedm.com.

16. PNC information comes from an interview with John Demarchis, June 10, 2013.

Chapter 5

1. Telephone interview with Tim Riley and other USAA personnel, February 13, 2013.

2. SAS, *2013 Big Data Survey Research Brief*, p. 1, http://www.sas.com/resources/whitepaper/wp_58466.pdf.

3. Telephone interview with Allen Naidoo, March 26, 2013.

4. Telephone interview of an executive (who did not wish to be named) with Jill Dyché, March 2013.

5. *Cisco Visual Networking Index: Global Mobile Data Traffic Forecast Update*, February 6, 2013, http://www.cisco.com/en/US/solutions/collateral/ns341/ns525/ns537/ns705/ns827/white_paper_c11-520862.html.

Chapter 6

1. Interview with Tim Riley and Shannon Gilbert on February 13, 2013.

2. Tasso Argyros, in various informal conversations in 2013.

3. Information on LinkedIn and People You May Know comes from a telephone interview with Jonathan Goldman, an in-person interview with Reid Hoffman, and discussions with DJ Patil, all in 2012.

4. Information about Nora Denzel and Intuit comes from an interview by the author with George Roumeliotis, February 2012, and from Bruce Upbin, "How Intuit Uses Big Data for the Little Guy," *Forbes.com*, April 26, 2012, http://www.forbes.com/sites/bruceupbin/2012/04/26/how-intuit-uses-big-data-for-the-little-guy/.

5. In-person and e-mail discussions with Murli Buluswar, March 2013.

6. E-mail discussion with Zoher Karu, April 25, 2013.

7. Reid Hoffman, blog post, http://reidhoffman.org/if-why-and-how-founders-should-hire-a-professional-ceo/.

8. A good description of the role of automation in financial services, and its historical rise, is in Christopher Steiner, *Automate This: How Algorithms Came to Rule Our World* (New York: Portfolio, 2012).

9. Information about the Heathrow application comes from interviews with Pegasystems executives; the Pegasystems website (www.pegasystems.com); and Justin Kern, "Heathrow Lands BPM for On-Time Flights," *Information Management*, December 11, 2012, http://www.information-management.com/news/Heathrow-Lands-BPM-for-On-Time-Flights-10023650-1.html.

Chapter 7

1. Jeffrey Dean and Sanjay Ghemewat, "MapReduce: Simplified Data Processing on Large Clusters," December 2004, http://research.google.com/archive/mapreduce.html.

2. Jeanne G. Harris, Allan Alter, and Christian Kelly, "How to Run IT at the Speed of Silicon Valley," *Wall Street Journal* blog post, May 14, 2013, http://blogs.wsj.com/cio/2013/05/14/how-to-run-it-at-the-speed-of-silicon-valley/.

3. E-mail correspondence with Christopher Ahlberg, May 26, 2013.

4. Discussion panel and e-mail correspondence with Jim Davis, May–June 2013.

5. A/B testing is described in Brian Christian, "The A/B Test: Inside the Technology That's Changing the Rules of Business," *Wired*, April 25, 2012, http://www.wired.com/business/2012/04/ff_abtesting/.

6. I describe eBay's testing, and the process of doing business experiments in general, in "How to Design Smart Business Experiments," *Harvard Business Review*, February 2009, 68–76.

7. Claire Cain Miller and Catherine Rampell, "Yahoo Orders Home Workers Back to the Office," *New York Times*, February 25, 2013, www.nytimes.com/2013/02/26/technology/yahoo-orders-home-workers-back-to-the-office.html.

8. Natasha Singer, "If My Data Is an Open Book, Why Can't I Read It?" *New York Times*, May 25, 2013, http://www.nytimes.com/2013/05/26/technology/for-consumers-an-open-data-society-is-a-misnomer.html.

9. See Danny Dover, "The Evil Side of Google? Exploring Google's User Data Collection," (blog post) for an outdated, but still impressive and scary, list of the user data collected by Google in 2008, at http://www.seomoz.org/blog/the-evil-side-of-google-exploring-googles-user-data-collection.

10. Arun Murthy, HortonWorks blog post, http://hortonworks.com/blog/moving-hadoop-beyond-batch-with-apache-yarn/#.UjyFW2RASe0.

11. IBM Corporation, "What Is Hadoop" website, http://www-01.ibm.com/software/data/infosphere/hadoop/.

12. Gil Press, "Top 10 Most Funded Big Data Start-ups," *Forbes* blog post, March 18, 2013, http://www.forbes.com/sites/gilpress/2013/03/18/top-10-most-funded-big-data-startups/.

13. Cynthia Kocialski, "The Story Behind a Big Data Startup's Success," blog post, May 21, 2013, http://cynthiakocialski.com/blog/2013/05/21/successful-entrepreneur-raul-valdes-perez-tells-his-startup-story/.

Chapter 8

1. NewVantage Partners, *Big Data Executive Survey: Themes and Trends*, 2012.

2. Peter Evans and Marco Annunziata, "*Industrial Internet: Pushing the Boundaries of Minds and Machines*," GE report, November 26, 2012, www.ge.com/docs/chapters/Industrial_Internet.pdf.

3. *Big Data: The Next Frontier for Innovation, Competition, and Creativity*, McKinsey Global Institute, 2011.

4. David Floyer (originating author), *Financial Comparison of Big Data MPP Solution and Data Warehouse Appliance*; for the complete story on this study, see http://wikibon.org/wiki/v/Financial_Comparison_of_Big_Data_MPP_Solution_and_Data_Warehouse_Appliance.

5. SAS 2013 Big Data Survey, http://www.sas.com/resources/whitepaper/wp_58466.pdf.

6. Gil Press has published a concise history of data science in a *Forbes* blog post; see "A Very Short History of Data Science," *Forbes.com*, May 28, 2013, http://www.forbes.com/sites/gilpress/2013/05/28/a-very-short-history-of-data-science/.

Appendix

1. Erik Brynjolfsson and Andy McAfee, "Is Your Company Ready for Big Data?," *Harvard Business Review* website, http://hbr.org/web/2013/06/assessment/is-your-company-ready-for-big-data.

Index

Note: Page numbers followed by *f* refer to figures; page numbers followed by *t* refer to tables.